Mundane Journeys
Through an Amazing World

Michael R Bissell

www.michaelbissell.com.
Printed in the United States of America

Publisher's Cataloging-in-Publication data:

Bissell, Michael
Mundane Journeys (Through an Amazing World) / Michael R. Bissell --1st Edition
p. cm.
ISBN 978-1514196694 (Paperback)

1. Travel I. Title

Book Design by Michael R. Bissell

For four generations of women in my family:

My grandmother Jane who wrote for a living,
My mother Jane who taught me to write,
My sister Cathy who showed it was possible
And my niece Kyra who wouldn't let it go

And, of course, for Markie, who suffered twice, once when I abandoned her
for my travels and once again when I abandoned her while writing about them

Prologue

The midafternoon flight from Spokane to Portland was half empty; while there is no first-class section on the little turboprops, I had both seats to myself. Lifting the armrest I spread out comfortably with both legroom and elbowroom. Practically first class.

The plane was flying low over the high desert of Eastern Washington making the details of the landscape recognizable as opposed to the soft quilt of green-and-brown earth and grey blotches of cities you usually see from the air. The sun was low in the west, framed below by the silhouette of the Cascades and above by a perfect balance of sky and clouds. Gold and red sunlight cast shadows inside the plane.

As I opened my book, I sipped a glass of wine that had been grown, fermented and aged on the same plot of land in the valley below, and I thought about the golden era of air travel when you knew you were flying and you felt special because it was magical.

And for that one flight, it was the golden era again.

Accidental Tourist

I HAD A COLLEAGUE IN THE FIRST INTERNET BOOM WHO WAS invited to speak at a conference in Barcelona He got on a plane in Portland, Oregon on a Saturday night, got to Barcelona late Sunday, slept, spoke at the conference Monday morning, and flew back. He saw a few airports, a hotel lobby and conference room and little else. He had flown to Spain, but somehow never actually went there.

I have a friend who flies to exotic places and orders gin and tonics with cocktail onions and proceeds to sit by the pool for a week reading. Then he flies home again. That isn't travel even if it is a great vacation.

Over the years I have driven across the U.S. a couple of times, and I've flown hundreds of thousands of miles to visit a lot of windowless conference rooms to talk about abstract technologies. If I let the destination shape my view of the world, there were still some amazing conference rooms.

But the journey is the destination -- wherever you go, there is always something to look at. And in this book I try to describe a few of those mundane places that might not be as mundane as all that.

Prologue 4
   Accidental Tourist 5
Interstate 80 9
   My Hometown 10
   Nevada 14
   The Middle of Nowhere 19
   Of Midwestern Seas and Castles...25
   The Other I-80: Pennsylvania 28
Urban America 33
   New York, New York 34
   South Beach Florida 39
   Washington D.C. 44
Living in Americana 55
   A Hundred Miles from Cincinnati 56
   The Not So Deep South 63
   Vegas, Baby! 70
Oregon 77
   The Other Portland 78
   Bicycling the Cascades..90
   The Dry Side 98
California...103
   The North Coast 104
   The Sea Ranch 111
   Beaches, Softball and Oil Rigs 114
   Death Valley...117
Nowhere Lands..119
   The Glamour of Travel...120
Anglophile's Paradise 129
   London 130
   Manchester...141
   Liverpool 147
   The Wall at Chester 152
   English Dancing in the English Countryside 157
The Nordic Experience 161
   Norway 162
   Sweden...172

Iceland..181
Foreign Lands 189
   Tokyo 190
   Bangalore...202
Interlude...213
Epilogue 214

Interstate 80

The cornfields had been going for what felt like days. After crossing four states, Nebraska never seemed to end. More miles of corn. Another rest area. More corn. Then I saw the cloud coming up on the side of the road.

"SILAGE!!!"

The Mate on the Titanic screaming "ICEBERG" couldn't have been more terrified when he shouted his similar warning. We quickly rolled up the windows and braced for the worst as the cloud of rotten old feed and vegetation that smelled as if it had been through an entire pig farm enveloped the truck. The smell was unbearable as the sun was blotted out.

After emerging from the dark stench, we rolled the windows down again, trying in vain to vent the smell from the truck, but it was too late, it was stuck in our noses and stuck in our memories so even when there was nothing left, we could still smell it.

My Hometown

WHEN PEOPLE ASK ME WHERE I'M FROM I TELL THEM, "Interstate 80." I was born in Napa, but grew up in towns along the freeway in Northern California. As a kid, I always had a fantasy that I would someday get in a car and drive all the way to the other end of that freeway.

The road is more than just a long band of asphalt and concrete that runs from San Francisco to New York City; it's a portal to other worlds. It is simultaneously easy and impossible to imagine it rolling across the country because it's a local, mundane thing that somehow becomes magical when it transports you to another place -- like when the wardrobe takes you to Narnia.

It still seems strange when I see a sign for I-80 in Pennsylvania; to me, I-80 is a California freeway. The signage, the interchanges, even the pavement is different in different states. But seeing signs for I-80 in other cities is like running into an old high-school friend in some random city far away.

My personal bit of freeway is the stretch of I-80 from San Francisco to Reno which I know like some people know their old neighborhood, because for me, it *is* the old neighborhood. I find that things have changed here and there when I go back to visit... there's a new bridge in the Bay and at the Carquinez Straits, Fairfield has absorbed more farmland, and the Nut Tree is a shopping center, but the place is the same.

It's funny to think of having personal and family history with a freeway. My grandmother did hard news back in the 1930s, and she smoked and drank with the best of them in the office and kept up with the guys' shenanigans. Back before there was an I-80 and back before anything other than ferries crossed the bay, the guys from the newsroom talked each other into sneaking out onto the girders of the Bay Bridge while it was being built and, naturally, my grandmother went along.

The giant road decks weren't in place yet and there was nothing but air and seagulls between them and the waters of the San Francisco Bay below. I've done plenty of stupid things that could have killed me, but then I think about how my grandmother could have slipped, even in sensible shoes, damning a whole generation of descendants to oblivion, let alone being given a chance to poke an eye out.

Years later we would shuttle back and forth along the freeway between Berkeley and Sacramento. To a six-year-old, a hundred miles was an eternity, but today I drive through the dull brown hills with their sparse oak trees and feel an emotional pang. Cordelia is far from the most romantic place I've ever been, but even with its sprawling shopping centers, I get a wistful feeling when I pass through. Nostalgia is stupid that way -- you can't control what's going to trigger it.

Then there's the long, straight shot of freeway in the Sacramento Valley, sometimes separated by oleander bushes, sometimes just by a steel cable. Vacaville gives way to open farmland and Dixon gives way to Davis and then Sacramento rises above the spillway where the flooding river has been diverted and rice is grown in huge, artificial wetlands.

Crossing the causeway into Sacramento feels like entering an ancient, fortified city. The only way into the city is over the three-mile bridge and levee system with the long, familiar {*thump*}-[*pause*]-{*thump*}-[*pause*]-{*thump*}-[*pause*] of the tires crossing the seams in the bridge. The rice and corn fields extend to the horizon in the south, while the towers of downtown Sacramento rise in the east.

There was a time you could ride your bicycle on a separate strip of asphalt in the spillway below. I would get a weird "sneaking into the city" feeling as I rode on a thin strip of pavement through dusty fields while paralleling the towering causeway. Eventually they built a bike lane on the freeway alongside the hurtling cars and they then dug up the old bike lane, returning it to dirt and closing the break in the giant moat on Sacramento's western border.

Heading past Sacramento and into the Sierra Nevada Mountains makes me think of Hobbits going to Buckland. When we were kids we would visit my mother's Aunt Kay in Dutch Flat, the somewhat removed relations in a somewhat removed part of the world that was still part of the place I grew up with, but just far enough away to feel like a bit of an adventure.

Dutch Flat is in the foothills of the Sierras where the leafy trees and dirt haven't completely given way to the lodgepoles and granite of the real mountains. But you are clearly out of the valley -- the tap water is sweet and the air is clean.

You hardly notice the smoke and dirt when you are breathing it in the Sacramento Valley. Rising out of the valley into the clean air of the foothills means that when you drive back you see the smear of smog ahead and below you. And you know that you have to descend back into it eventually.

Turning your back on the brown grasses and the brown air of the valley, you head up and into the lands where the Sierra Nevada Mountains truly begin. The red firs and lodgepole pines start to crowd the shoulder of the freeway, and the elevation signs seem to come more and more frequently.

Our trips in the winter to play in the snow would always start with the anticipation of the first sight of snow. Whoever saw it first would yell out "Snow!" as we saw the first patch of white, and then another patch would appear, and very quickly after that, the snow would overwhelm the terrain.

The last time I drove up I-80 past Sacramento, however, was in mid-September in a twenty-year-old Ford F-150 and towing the biggest U-Haul trailer they make. As cold and snowy as my childhood memories of the climb were, the Sierras in September are hot. And an old truck, straining to pull a trailer filled with everything my wife and I owned made the temperature gauge skyrocket.

The seemingly endless grade ground on, and the truck went slower and slower as the needle on the temperature gauge climbed. You know it's bad when semis start to pass you, and eventually I had to pull over on the broad shoulder of the freeway where, in the wintertime, families on their way to a snowy holiday would chain up.

At 6,000 feet the thin air doesn't wick away as much heat from the engine as the moist air at sea level. And in September, it's still in the 80s even high up in the Sierras, so the wait was long, trying to stay cool in the cab of the truck, listening to the whoosh of cars that could fly by without the annoyance of overheating.

Eventually the truck cooled enough and I was able to get underway again and over Donner Pass. The cool water of Donner Lake looked like a wonderful place to stop, but I think I'll always have a problem with staying at a resort named after a group of pioneers who ignored the warnings, got stuck in the snow and ate the dead bodies of their comrades and family.

The landscape starts to get more barren heading down into Reno and I find myself on the edge of the known universe of the Interstate 80 I knew as a child -- it was as far as we would go on vacations and snow trips. We weren't even that curious. It was the edge of the world, and I just assumed there was nothing until New York.

I could never imagine what was really out there.

Nevada

THE BARREN LANDSCAPES OF ICELAND AND UTAH ARE destinations for movie makers who want to film otherworldly places. Nevada also has barren rocks and desolate spaces, but it somehow isn't pretty enough to be another planet in the movies.

Even so, Nevada is probably more like what a human colony on another planet would really look like. The lifeless landscape is punctuated with industrial plumes on the horizon where they extract minerals from the rock and convert those minerals into some complex chemicals used in some toxic process that produces other strange materials, many of which end up in children's toys and military weapons.

After leaving Reno, the freeway winds through low hills of gravel and rock. The rare and scattered communities feel like terraforming experiments that haven't quite taken root. Small, gnarled trees huddle close to functional buildings and small green plots grow incongruously in the expanse of open plains that are dotted with dark, scrubby local bushes -- vegetation that looks alien to my eye but are actually native plants that can endure this extreme environment without a garden hose.

Sometime in the middle of the night I felt the rumble of the tires crossing a cattle guard as I rolled into Lovelock for gas. The town gave me the impression of a walled encampment in the Wild West, but the fences and city gates weren't keeping out the native people -- they were defending the town from an onslaught of invasive herbivores.

It obviously wasn't working; the heavy smell of cow dung was everywhere. The gasoline fumes escaping my tank as I filled the truck weren't enough to counteract the reeking manure outside the city gates. Even the brightly lit, air conditioned mini-mart at the gas station had that... sniff... smell.

Here, in the middle of the night, in a brightly lit gas station market, steeped in the smell of cattle and manure, I played my first quarter in a slot machine. And I won an entire dollar. This turned out to be the last time I ever won at a slot machine, and it just makes the place seem a little more like purgatory -- the stench of hell tempered by Coke products and the small satisfaction from a sinful game.

About 70 miles up the highway of brush and rock and gravel is Winnemucca. When I stumble on a town in the middle of nowhere I always wonder what people do to make money in a place three hours from a major city (and a major airport). I assume there are ranchers and miners and chemists and truck drivers. I'm guessing there aren't many feng shui consultants. Money in Winnemucca is earned.

I've actually been to Winnemucca twice -- once in my cross-country move with the pickup truck and once when returning from a conference in Colorado, driving a Toyota Scion covered in vinyl advertising and a cartoon super hero flying out the side. It was an absurd vehicle; children would wave at me like I was part of the circus, and I particularly remember filling up somewhere in Idaho while a local cowboy watched.

He finally came up to me and said, "Well, that's... {long pause}... Eye catching." I still want to know what the series of adjectives were that flipped through his mind before he settled on, "eye catching."

Winnemucca butts right up against BLM land, and Google told me there was a campground just four miles out of town. I was keeping my costs low on my trip in the Scion and camping along the way so I headed out of town away from I-80 in search of a moderate night's stay.

The route took me through the small suburban neighborhood in Winnemucca (there's only one). Then the houses abruptly ended -- there were a few ranchettes and then just rock and scrub. My cartoon-clad car started to look even more absurd as the asphalt turned to gravel and I wound around low hills and past dry gullies.

Just when I was about to give up, I came to the BLM sign and the edge of the recreation area. As I pulled in I found the ground burnt to a cinder all around the campground. Some wildfire had come through and consumed what little vegetation there had been, leaving a thin layer of black ashes behind.

Fortunately the area with the poured-concrete picnic table was clear of ashes and any anything else. It's odd that the definition of "primitive campground" includes a road, a parking area and a picnic table but no water or bathrooms.

There was a pit toilet, and I once again found myself being grateful for having male plumbing -- sitting in that dark, putrid chamber would have been something even CIA interrogators at Guantanamo would have found cruel and unusual.

The night was calm and warm enough that I didn't need to pitch a tent, but I had heard enough horror stories of snakes and scorpions and other creatures of the night, so sleeping on the bare ground was out. Instead I unrolled my pad and sleeping bag onto the smooth concrete surface of the picnic table.

With the charred hills and the moonless night making everything feel even darker, I stretched out on the stone surface. I felt like I was the only living creature in a deathly underworld laying down atop my own crypt. That is, until the lights of a pickup truck towing ATVs washed over me... Maybe they were minions of a dark lord up in the canyon. Or maybe they were just Nevadans heading out into a place that I saw as deathly and spooky, but they saw as a playground.

Heading east from Winnemucca takes you through more miles of vast open country, more scrubby plants and, eventually, the city of Elko. Elko is a low spot on the freeway, and not just metaphorically. It's dusty and gritty and while it's twice as big as Winnemucca, it somehow feels smaller, even more cut off from the rest of the world way out into the empty lands of Nevada.

I swung off the freeway into town to fill the tank. Even though the gas station was in town, it had those poorly defined borders where the asphalt fades into the dirt, and the trucks that turn too widely don't seem to notice or care that they have left the paved surface.

A huge, dark cloud was forming in the distance on the other side of the town. At first I thought it would bring welcome rain, but as the wind picked up and the darkness spread from the other end of the valley, I could tell this wasn't going to be a gentle summer shower.

The dust storm came across the city like something from an apocalyptic Hollywood movie. A nearly solid wall of roiling, dark cloud was blotting out the hills, the scrub, the city and, of course, the sky. I half expected to see dark horsemen riding on the tendrils of dust that shot out of the clouds like trails from another, darker, universe.

The gas station attendant didn't seem too worried about the impending doom, but I finished filling up and got on the freeway as quickly as I could -- the storm must have been extremely localized, perhaps a curse for the inmates of Elko, because I was soon back out in the sunshine with the warm brown hills and the friendly plants in a landscape that had seemed so desolate less than an hour before.

Just as I started to find some comfort in the arid empty land of Nevada, I came to West Wendover -- there isn't much way to tell where Nevada's West Wendover ends and Utah's Wendover begins, other than the casinos. They say the casino and resort are filled with wayward Mormons who have slipped out of Utah's 3.2% beer laws and clean living to spend a little time, and a little more money, to see what life is like on the wild side.

But those of us on the long drive from somewhere though nowhere are forced to stop here for gas (and forced to walk the entire length of a casino to use the bathroom). With the jagged mountains of Nevada at my back, I looked out over an enormous plain of grey and white and tan, flat as far as the eye can see. And, unlike the 400 miles back to Reno, before me was 120 miles of truly lifeless, alien land -- the Great Salt Plain.

The Middle of Nowhere

SLC IS A HUB FOR DELTA, SO I'VE SEEN THE GREAT SALT LAKE and the Great Salt Plain from the air more times than I remember.

The edge of the lake is a bizarre sight from the air -- a patchwork of levees have created isolated pools of striking color. The deep azure water is what you would expect to see in a salty lake. But then, directly on the other side of a levee is bright purple water, and next to that, a rich, bright green. Algae and bacteria can live in the salty water, and they colonize the lagoon with their kin, much like the Mormons in the city that bears the lake's name.

I-80 runs east of the Great Salt Lake through the Salt Plains -- wide-open expanses of salt spanning hundreds of miles that stop suddenly at the craggy feet of the mountains in Nevada.

You've seen the Salt Plains in countless commercials with cars whipping across a white plain, or a scientist standing in the emptiness explaining how this gleaming appliance stands on its own. It inspires minimalist photography and surreal scenes in movies where reality has been shattered.

Seen on the screen, it looks almost inviting. Seen through the windows of a car, it is awe-inspiring. Seen from a horse-drawn wagon it must have been slowly terrifying.

When rushing down I-80 on smooth asphalt with air conditioning and surround-sound stereo it's hard to believe that people once made this trek on foot and by wagon. Twenty miles a day on foot is a good pace, and if they took the route I-80 takes today, they would be in the salt for at least 10 days.

But the Salt Plain isn't completely unrelieved. There are hills that look like islands in the sea of white. They are just as lifeless as the salt-laden land around them, but at least they are made of dirt and the dull brown rising above the plain is something of a relief compared to the glaring white of the plains.

I crossed this plain one stormy afternoon in the cartoon-clad Toyota Scion, a bright speck of blue in an ocean of salty white. My laptop, randomly shuffling through gigabytes of music, was tied into the sound system of the car. The sunlight breaking through the clouds was dark red and orange, and the sharp peaks of the mountains in the distance took on an even more foreboding, sinister look as the clouds streamed around them, making me think of the dark lands of fantasy.

Then the music shuffled into a haunting operatic piece by Vangelis with deep, throbbing bass tones over which a soaring, sad soprano wailed. It felt like being in one of those art-house films that people talk about for years as they try to define the emotion that the scene evoked.

Sometimes life imitates art because so much art strives to imitate moments like this.

Escaping the Salt Plain means entering the treacherous roads of Salt Lake City. It's a tough town to drive through in the best of conditions, darting around in a small, late model, if absurd, car. But the first time I drove through the Crossroads of the West I was in the old pickup truck hauling the extra-long trailer and it was downright dangerous.

You may be thinking, "The city of Joseph Smith is more dangerous than the winds of Nevada? More dangerous than the climbs in the Sierras?" This isn't a terrain or weather issue, this is People.

Driving through Salt Lake at rush hour brings out all the people. While there are 200,000 people in Salt Lake City, there are very few people *from* Salt Lake. I believe this is because so many Mormons come from all over the world and bring their different driving styles with them -- and those styles don't mix.

In Boston you have to wait a couple of heartbeats after the lights change because one or two cars on the cross street blast through the red light as it changes. In San Francisco, you stop on the yellow, because when the light changes in the other direction there's someone turning left bolting into the intersection the microsecond their light turns green.

Now take both those driving styles and put them in one city. Put the Ohio drivers who think that your turn indicator means they need to close the gap so you can't change lanes. Take the Oregonians who are so polite they'll break the law to give you the right of way. Take every driving style from all over the US and around the world and put them in one city.

And that's Salt Lake City.

There is no way to know what the car next to you is going to do. It may speed up, it may slow down. Hell, it may slam on its brakes and do a 180 and head back the other way. And when you're driving a slightly underpowered truck with a slightly overloaded trailer... it's terrifying.

Just east of Salt Lake City it gets even more terrifying. Going from Parley's Canyon at about 4,500 feet to Parley's Summit at over 7,000 feet in just 13 miles through deep, winding canyons makes that climb over the Sierra Nevadas seem pleasant by comparison.

Grinding up the grade in the old truck with the big load was hard enough. Barely able to pass the semis at 35 miles per hour, the old truck survived the climb only because it was about 20 degrees cooler than it had been in the Sierras.

But the story about coming back down that same canyon a couple of years later takes skipping ahead on I-80 and working our way back...

When I first drove east on I-80, Wyoming seemed like the Garden of Eden. After the scrubland of Nevada, the Great Salt Plain, and the rocky canyons of Utah, Wyoming seemed lush and green.

Coming back across the same terrain a few years later I learned that the term "God's Country" is relative. Wyoming is just as empty and just as desolate as Nevada, albeit with recognizable grasslands rather than alien scrub. Nevada still had traffic and commerce, but Wyoming is a great empty land, what we really think of when we say "fly-over state."

In the winter this long, rolling prairie can become dangerous country. I had always thought the Interstate system was somehow immune to weather, but in Wyoming they have gates from town to town that they close when the snow becomes so deep and so impassable that the Interstate is erased from the surface of the Earth.

There are no real cities between Salt Lake City and Cheyenne. There are small towns like Rawlins (where I found a Thai restaurant with plates and glasses from IKEA, showing the signs of globalization in the Far West), but for the most part the freeway rolls for miles through cattle country. There will be an exit in the middle of nowhere with a sign saying something like, "Next Exit: 40 Miles." Only that next exit is marked "Ranch Road" with no ranch in sight.

Somewhere out in this empty country is the world's largest gas station where they claim to have more gas pumps than anyone, anywhere. There's a hotel, a campground, a market and all the services anyone could hope for (including showers for the truckers).

The story goes that back in the settler days a man found shelter in a little valley during one of those blowing snowstorms that will shut down the Interstate today. He vowed to come back and establish a rest house for other tired travellers, and today that rest house is Little America -- truck stop of the gods.

Travelling from east to west through this country with a different pickup truck and an equally large trailer, I had mapped out the stops in the prairie like Little America. This was before everyone had a cell phone, and before there was coverage on every mile of the Interstate System. Mile after mile of cattle country. Mile after mile of Ranch Road exits. Signs with penguins advertising Little America. It was slow going and truck stops were golden oases that I found myself looking forward to like a settler in a prairie schooner would the isolated trading posts.

The road west of Little America is more of the same until crossing into Utah where the world gets stonier and drier. Passing through Park City, which is less of a town and more of a ski resort and nearly vacant in the summer, I slowly climbed the east side of the range and finally reached the top of Parley's Summit.

In a modern car you crawl to the top of a mountain and then you get to enjoy the speed of coasting down the other side. But when you're driving an over-loaded truck, you have to go just as slowly down the other side as well, or risk losing control and rolling off the road.

The semis go down the hill at about 30 miles per hour. I took it a little faster at about 40, passing the big rigs at a slow but steady pace.

With a loud bang the steering suddenly started jerking and the truck was bumping around as one of the tires blew out on the truck.

I quickly downshifted while pumping the brakes trying to merge back into the right lane without colliding with the slow-moving, big trucks. If I had been driving an automatic I don't know that I would have been able to slow down before the next corner in the canyon came up. Bumping and shuddering I got the truck and trailer over to the shoulder where I held onto the steering wheel for a couple of minutes trying to get my heart back under control.

Keep in mind that I had just driven through some of the emptiest country in the U.S. No cell signal. No towns. No phones. No chance for help if something happened -- something like a tire blowing out on an overloaded truck.

Once I convinced myself I was safe and alive, I looked around. Over the low, simple wire fence was the clubhouse for a golf course. And right out front, plain as could be, was a phone booth. Of all the places I could have been stuck, a restaurant and a phone booth were pretty far down the list.

Fortunately I had AAA and after I slipped through the fence and called for service, I grabbed a sandwich. Soon the service truck showed up with a floor jack. He was able to lift the rear of the truck with the trailer still attached (something I would never have risked with my scissor jack) and swap out the rim with a fringe of what used to be a tire for the spare.

That night was spent in the Little America hotel in Salt Lake City. The hot tub and the pool helped release the knots that had formed in my shoulders while gripping the wheel, but the new tire that I bought and had installed that night did far more when it came to a sense of relief and safety.

Of Midwestern Seas and Castles

THE ROAD SKIMMED ABOVE THE FLAT, BROWN SEA, WITH EAST and west traffic separated by a small canal of murky water. I raced along at 60 miles an hour surrounded by a light but steady flow of cars and trucks that found themselves inexplicably far out to sea while on an Interstate freeway.

Occasionally an overpass would rise out of the waters like an abstract piece of industrial art; inevitably there would be an abandoned car sitting on the span with nowhere to go but the murky waters of the Mississippi-Missouri Sea.

Spring rain had come to the Midwest after heavy snowfall, and as the rain fell and the snow melted, the waters rose. In some places the levees didn't get the opportunity to break open, but were overcome by the sheer height of the rivers. Entire towns were flooded, landmarks erased by the rising muddy water, turning the Midwest into a featureless expanse of brown.

But the freeways rolled on.

The US freeway system started as part of a civil defense program back in the 1950s, and while some people still wonder if it was really to support the movement of troops in a Cold War world, or if it was to help promote the automobile culture of a post-war utopia that never really was, the history didn't matter. I-80 didn't so much as flinch as nine states succumbed to the rising waters.

In the light rain it was a surreal, but tranquil drive. Then the rain came in hard and fast; the highest speed of the wipers wasn't enough to clear the deluge from the windshield and the thunderous noise of rain pounding on the roof drowned out the engine, the radio and the *fip/fip/fip/fip/fip* of the wipers.

I could barely make out the white shoulder line that was keeping me from driving off the edge of the road and into the mud and water. But, to be honest, I was less worried about running off the road than running into a car in front of me. People rightfully panic and come to a dead stop when they can't see through a wall of water and can't hear over the deluge enveloping the universe. At the same time, I didn't want to stop moving for fear of someone plowing into the back of me.

Soon the rain slowed and I could hear the normal drag of the wipers and see the road again as it sliced through the Midwestern Sea. Eventually I came to the shore, if you could call the thinning water turning into a muddy field a "shore." And then the muddy fields turned back into the nondescript fields of grasses and grains that make up the country's midsection.

When not drowned in floodwaters, the place they call the Heartland of America doesn't have a lot going on. If I was going to pick a part of the body to compare to the Midwest, I would choose something like the Lower Back of America, or maybe the Hairy Belly of America. There's a lot of space and not a lot to look at.

From what I can tell the big attraction in Davenport, Iowa is the riverboat gambling on the Mississippi. But I found something different. At the gas station, with the buzz of June bugs in the air, looking past the coin-operated air machine and the generic mini-mart, rising above the dark leaves of trees in the Mississippi summer, there was a Tudor castle.

I'm not talking about one of those painted plasterboard things that looks like a McMansion but actually sells wine, cheese and cigarettes. No, this looked like the real deal. A tall tower rising above a rambling structure of stucco and dark wood on a large garden property.

It turned out a great deal of that garden property was paved for parking, but entering the castle from the bright summer heat was like stepping into the German Alps. The air conditioning gave the place a mountain chill and the subdued indoor lighting disappeared into dark wood and leather. Once my eyes adjusted from the Midwestern sun, I could see the high ceilings and deep alcoves with comfortable chairs surrounded by bookshelves.

Turning each corner found another large room -- there was a restaurant, a bar, a lobby, another sitting room... The establishment was a combination of hotel and destination restaurant, part of a family-owned chain that spread from Des Moines to Peoria.

I visited the one in Peoria later that day, and it was even better appointed. Dinner that night was veal schnitzel and strong German beer, not as incongruous as some meals I've had since, but I didn't really know about the huge German influence in the Midwest at the time. I didn't know that people ate schnitzel all the time in Peoria so, to me, it was an exotic meal in a strange locale.

But, I guess that over time, even schnitzel doesn't play in Peoria anymore. The Jumers chain has since fallen aside in favor of the big casino resort they built on the banks of the Mississippi. But for one odd afternoon, I found myself in Bavaria by the Mississippi.

The Other I-80: Pennsylvania

THERE ARE A FEW SECTIONS OF I-80 I HAVEN'T DRIVEN -- THE road from California to Cincinnati branched in Davenport, Iowa, taking a turn down through Peoria and Indianapolis. I rejoined I-80 on a trip from Cincinnati to Pennsylvania, pulling onto I-80 nearly 500 miles from Davenport in Cleveland, Ohio.

There is that brief bit of I-80 between Cleveland and Pennsylvania. I know you should never judge a town at 70 miles an hour along the freeway, but the industrial corridor of tire manufacturers and smelters and other buildings belching dark smoke does not bode well for Akron.

But almost as soon as you cross into Pennsylvania you find yourself in another world. Pennsylvania's I-80 is not the industrial I-80 of northeastern Ohio, and it's definitely not the same I-80 I grew up with.

It's hard to explain how one bit of freeway can look so much different than another bit of freeway. But like visiting your cousins where they serve peanut butter and banana sandwiches (no, I'm still not over that) it's just… different.

Unlike the asphalt of California, much of the Pennsylvania freeway is poured concrete. The exits aren't always overpasses; sometimes cross-streets come right up to the freeway, and the merging cars have to leap out to a bit of pavement in the middle of the two lanes of freeway, only to sit and wait for a chance to turn left into speeding traffic.

After so much flat land in the Midwest, Pennsylvania seems almost mountainous. Rolling hills are steep enough that they block the view of the next section of freeway and gentle woods climbing the hills give it a tamed wilderness feeling -- think of the outskirts of the Shire in *The Hobbit*. Everything is soft and gentle, but uncultivated. Nothing is going to kill you, but you still feel like you're "out in the land."

Filling up in the town of DuBois, (which I somehow knew without having to ask, was pronounced doo-Boyce by the locals), felt more like a tame version of *Deliverance*. It's not that these were really rough rednecks, it just felt… unsophisticated. While small towns are often charming because of their simple lives, DuBois was different, and I moved on.

Beyond DuBois and a little off I-80 is State College, Pennsylvania, home of Penn State and the birth of Doppler Radar. I had come to town to visit with Accuweather, otherwise I would probably never think of State College as the home of Doppler Radar but rather the town with the school where football is more important than reporting a coach who was molesting children in the showers.

And to the small town of State College, Penn State football probably is more important. I was there during the whole Sandusky thing and every shop window in the town had signs saying, "We support Penn State Football!" When you compare State College and DuBois it's easy to see why Penn State football is so important; State College is a thriving town with grand old houses, a historic downtown and modern cuisine while DuBois is dull concrete, WalMart and a Denny's.

The hotel I was staying in was around a hundred dollars or so for a night. It was a basic, four story affair without a restaurant or a bar. The rooms were the standard bathroom in the entry hall, big bed, a big TV, a small work desk and a view of the parking lot.

While standing in the lobby, waiting for a ride, I heard the registration desk clerk on the phone. "$499 is the best rate I can give you that night... Yes, well, that's the weekend of the Penn State/Ohio Game... No sir, I assume all the hotels are probably booked that night... Yes... this is one of our lower rates... Okay, what's your credit card number?"

Five hundred bucks will get you a pretty nice room in most posh hotels in the world. And yet, this small, middle of the road hotel that was barely even a step up from a motel, could command that rate when Penn State played.

But Penn State isn't just football. Not to be confused with the Ivy League school, Penn State still has its collection of ivory tower inhabitants.

I had found a tap room right off campus from Penn State with enough variety and quality to slake my Northwestern thirst for beer. It was difficult to see the bartender behind the collection of tap handles, but like a bibliophile in a bookstore eschewing the store directory, I would rather peruse the taps then read the menu.

A couple of twenty-somethings were having one of those conversations that college kids are having in bars around the world at any given time. It's the old back and forth that never goes anywhere because it never really gets going.

"I say the improbability of God makes it extremely unlikely that He exists," the woman was saying.

"But the fact you can't disprove His existence means that He might exist..."

I have a fairly standard argument that I can toss in on the "does God exist in the bar?" question. A slight clearing of my throat and a, "May I?" and I inserted the logical questions of birth defects, recreation centers built next to a sewage treatment plant and the fact we eat, breathe and vomit all through the same hole and I was "in."

While this was a college pub in a college town, it was still a town in rural Pennsylvania. The bartender was a local boy who had spent six years in the Navy. He helped maintain power plants aboard aircraft carriers and was struggling to get his bachelor's degree at Penn State.

Meanwhile, the philosophical couple were both finishing up their graduate degrees in geology and were struggling with the fact that they were indentured to their student loans, and the only real place they could work was with large oil companies --

something that would require abandoning their love of the pursuit of intellectualism.

The unfairness of the two extremes was blatant; here are two people with advanced degrees who have to take jobs they don't want, and the guy serving them beer probably has had more life experience and more practical education, but he has to serve beer because he doesn't have the right kind of education.

The value of bachelor's degrees is metaphysical; you have to believe the degrees are valuable. Like the argument I stumbled into on the existence of God, it takes faith to believe that a degree is important to your journey as a human being. Changing that belief structure is less about legislation and more about culture and accepting that the Navy Engineer may have more skills than the Penn State grad student.

But I believe that until we value the things people learn outside the books and lecture halls, we aren't really learning anything at all. Taprooms and battleships are excellent centers of education.

State College is not like other towns in Central Pennsylvania. When my wife and I celebrated our first anniversary, we drove from Cincinnati to spend a week in a small town north of I-80 called Eagles Mere.

This is the rural Pennsylvania people imagine. Not the concrete and gas stations of DuBois, not the bustle of State College with one-way streets and traffic lights, Eagles Mere has the rural simplicity of small town USA. It is comforting and relaxing by being off the beaten path in both location and how it felt to be lost in time.

Back in the day there was a rail line from New York City that ran into the Lost Mountains of Pennsylvania. The small lake by Eagles Mere hosted the wealthy from New York in guest houses and hotels which have since faded into a sleepy, summer retreat with small houses scattered around the lake.

The Eagles Mere Inn was on the American Plan, which meant they served breakfast and dinner, but you were on your own for lunch. In the village (really too small to be called a town) we found a bookstore that sold used hardcover library books at an amazing discount.

We spent our days sipping iced coffees on the wrap-around deck reading our newfound books, or paddling around the quiet lake in a rented canoe. It was the kind of place you read about, but you never really expect to find.

It's still hard for me to believe that such a tranquil place exists just a few hours down the freeway from one of the most intense cities on the planet. Having wound through mountains and deserts, cities and cornfields, Interstate 80 is close to its eastern terminus in the rolling hills of Pennsylvania.

I-80 technically comes to its end when it hits I-95 in New Jersey, but I like to think it really ends just a few miles further down the road in a place that is the exact opposite of wrap-around porches and quiet days reading and canoeing. The end of the road is New York City.

Urban America

Watching the snow blow by the window gave me the impression I was on a train; the aft lights shot around the landing gear to cast shadows below the plane that looked like train track rails while the bright lights on the wings created a tunnel of light making the horizontal, blowing snow look more like a close-by cutting in a hillside in Northern England. The thrumming of the jet engines vibrated the hull giving me the sensation of a railcar gliding over the tracks.

The thump of all three sets of wheels hitting the ground all at once was jarring and the plane began to slide left and right as the pilot killed the speed by reversing the engines. There was a terrifying moment when the engines wailed and the plane lurched forward, probably caught by the strong, shearing wind. But then the noise settled and we rolled over packed snow towards the gate.

It was going to be a long, cold week in Detroit.

New York, New York

KARL PILKINGTON WAS FORCED TO TRAVEL TO EXOTIC PLACES by Ricky Gervais in *An Idiot Abroad*. When shown a photo of the carved rock face that is the amazing Treasury of Petra in Jordan, he said, "I wouldn't want to live in that, I'd rather live in the cave across the way because then I would be able to look at that. The fellow that lives in that has to look at my cave."

When I stay in Manhattan I become a cliff dweller, looking out my window into the deep canyon formed by the hotel and the surrounding buildings. But then I stayed in the Hyatt in Jersey City and had a stunning view of the towers of Manhattan across the Hudson. And, I wasn't even in a cave, but a nicer, and less expensive hotel than the cramped, dark places I had stayed in Manhattan.

At one point a gigantic cruise ship, looking like a skyscraper on its side, plowed its way down the river towards the sea, dwarfing the tugboats and ferries in the river and the towers on the island. To the south I could see the Statue of Liberty standing above the trees in Liberty Park, and looking north there was more city disappearing into the distance.

I took the ferry into Manhattan which, like a lot of New York experiences, is a bit, but not entirely gritty. The commuter ferries are like city busses on the water -- hard seats and dirty windows. I couldn't see much until I stood by the open door in the back of the ferry and looked out over the spray from the boat's wake where I could see a river that is definitely part of the city.

The Hudson River is a big, deep river -- not big like the lazy, muddy rivers of the Midwest, but big the way New York does big. Ferries crisscrossed the water along with sailboats, tugboats, commercial ships and the buzzing of tourist helicopters overhead.

When I arrived in Manhattan I found myself caught up in the tide of people deboarding the half-dozen ferries that inexplicably all docked at the same time. The current of humanity swept me into the city and away from the water, like being washed ashore and I found myself on the sidewalk, gasping for breath.

If arriving by ferry is like being washed ashore, arriving by subway is like coming through a water main as it pushes people through the pipes under high pressure. I've seen Mariachi bands, a reading of Shakespeare, an a capella rapping dance troupe and a lonely cowboy singer on the subway trains. And those are just the panhandling performers.

My first vision of New York was of two girls in bright, colorful Indian saris on the drab subway. No one gives you a second look in New York, no matter what. There was a frumpy, bored New Yorker dozing next to them who has seen so much she hardly sees anything at all anymore.

The trains connect in labyrinth-like subway stations where you find more street performers, food and shops, and even police stations. It's probably possible to live in the New York subway system and never see the light of day for your entire life, and it's entirely possible that there are people who do just that.

I have a theory that New Yorkers think of Portland, Oregon, as just another borough that they get to by subway. Grab a cup of Stumptown Coffee in Brooklyn, then take a train to JFK, change trains (well, actually board a plane), arrive in PDX, change trains again (this time getting on MAX) and get another cup of Stumptown Coffee in Portland.

Being a business traveller I have found myself climbing out of the subway in Midtown more often than any human being should, and for me that has only been a few times. There are people who do this every day of their lives like some Sisyphean task, doomed to repeat it forever.

Midtown is the dull business district where nothing is really going on in the middle of the city where nothing ever stops.

A connoisseur of nondescript 1970s architecture would have a great sightseeing trip in Midtown -- some giant alien is obviously collecting one building out of every business district in American cities and storing them here for later collection. I won't be surprised if some day the entire island lifts out of the water and flies into space to be put on display in a galactic museum under the title *Amusing Human Structures.*

It always helps to have a local to show you around, and Helen, my friend and colleague from my days tweeting as *Mad Men's* Roger Sterling (she was Betty Draper), suggested a play after my Midtown meetings. We met at the "tckts" building in Times Square.

The July heat and rain were a remarkable combination making the air feel like hot soup that you had to will yourself to press through; which at least served the purpose of keeping some of the throngs of tourists away. The signs declaring the Broadway shows, as always, were huge, bright and animated. It seemed they had taken every Disney film ever made and turned it into a Broadway musical -- gigantic renderings of Disney princesses and animals towered over Times Square.

We chose *Our Town*, a show that everyone seems to have seen so many times in high school and community productions it seems odd that I somehow hadn't ever seen it. The show was in a couple of hours, so Helen suggested a "quirky New York thing" -- Chinese massage.

Onto the subway and up to 76th street, through a small, poorly marked door, into a room divided by curtains. I knew my muscles were a mess from stress and injury, but that woman found knots I didn't know existed. She didn't speak English beyond "okay?" and "too hard?" It didn't really matter what I said, she continued to poke, push and pinch the knots and tight muscles, refusing to let any bit of tension stay in my body even if it killed me. And it nearly did, but in a very good way.

Then back on the subway, down to the West Village, where we found the theater. I am often surprised by the run-down look of buildings in New York. The city has a used feeling, not New at all.

But it doesn't matter if the buildings are a little run down -- the play was amazing. Minimalistic, until the very end, when the characters relive a day in a life with amazing detail. Words won't do it, you'll just have to go to New York and get a ticket. I later learned from a director friend that the production I saw is one of the most acclaimed stagings of *Our Town* and one of the more talked about plays in theater circles.

Of course, some may say that's just New York on a Thursday.

After the play, we went to a Japanese/Peruvian restaurant with sidewalk cafe seating and we were served by a Korean hipster girl. Dinner consisted of duck confit gyoza, an amazing roll of lobster and tuna, and a dessert that was layered with a whipped milk meringue, chopped mango, caramel ice cream and sake jelly. I'm not sure I want to know how they jellify sake, but it was amazing.

Every time I visit New York I find something new. But it always feels wrapped in the trappings of something old. A few years after our massage/theater/jellied sake adventure, I met with Helen again. This time near Gramercy Park in an old bar, the kind where New York businessmen would have three martini lunches.

It felt appropriate to have a Manhattan, and as we sipped our drinks in the dark wood booth surrounded by a battered old tile floor, Helen mentioned that she had a book release party to go to and invited me along.

The book party was in an apartment facing Gramercy Park -- high ceilings, small rooms, lots of people with heavy rimmed glasses, drinking wine and talking about other people and other people's books. I once again got that feeling of life imitating art because art imitates life.

It felt like a scene from a Woody Allen movie; I half expected to see him sitting in the corner in deep discussion with Diane Keaton about some neurotic episode.

I remember parties like this from my childhood in the '70s when my mother was finding the literary scene in Davis, California. Forty years later, on the other side of the continent I had a sense of *deja vu*. Sometimes life imitates life, and the literary parties I remember were microcosms of the New York parties, much like Portland is a borough of New York. It's not, but it is.

Growing up I never really understood the attraction of New York. It always looked like a grimy, crowded city in movies and TV, and it is a grimy, crowded city. But it's vibrant and alive with people thinking and doing and creating. I don't think I could handle the pace every day, but I think I understand the attraction.

I may find another cocktail as amazing as the one I found at the unmarked speakeasy in the West Village. I may find another store that exceeds Macy's amazing displays. I may see another play that will stay with me for the rest of my life.

But to have all these things and so much more crammed into such a concentrated space is something only New York can really boast.

South Beach Florida

FLORIDA IS NEW YORK'S OLD-FOLKS HOME. WELL, NOT ALL OF it. There's Orlando with Disney and Universal Studios, and then there's South Beach. Florida is a big place, so those cities are more like the rooms Grandma and Grandpa keep for when the kids come to visit; the "real" Floridians don't go there unless they have company.

I had a client in Orlando. Of all the cities where it's odd to travel for business, Orlando has to be the oddest. The food is geared to families visiting Disneyland and there isn't a decent dry martini for over two hundred miles; not exactly a place you want to be after a day of negotiating contracts and obligations.

The drive through Central Florida from Orlando to Miami is long and dull. The orange groves roll by, the grazing cattle are like grazing cattle anywhere. The massive landfill project was interesting to see, especially in an air-conditioned car with the outside air cut off. There are occasional rest stops with a gas station and mini-mart in an island between the two sides of the freeway -- obviously the only commerce here is from people passing through.

Eventually there are more cities and more traffic and then I was stuck on the elevated freeway in the stop and go traffic of Miami.

Miami is a schizophrenic town. It is poor, crime-ridden and dirty. Then I crossed the water on the long, low bridges over the Biscayne Bay and entered the dreamlike world of South Beach.

South Beach is opulent, expensive, and filled with beautiful people. As I paid for my vodka mojito and found I was spending 19 bucks, with a gratuity automatically included, it suddenly felt very foreign, perhaps the Mediterranean or maybe a club for wealthy South American crime lords, but not the Florida I had gotten to know in Orlando.

On the north end of South Beach is the remodeled Catalina Hotel with its ultra-postmodern white rugs, white paint and gleaming chrome. Although the room was tiny, it wasn't cheap. Fortunately my client was paying -- he had picked it based on the photos on the website and while everything looked like the website, the sense when standing in the actual hotel was a feeling of an aging building under a coat of fresh paint.

Eddie Izzard, the British executive-transvestite comedian, made fun of the lack of history in the U.S. by referencing the renovation projects of the old hotels in South Beach where they restore hotels to their "original 1930's splendor!" Yes, England has 2,000-year-old Roman walls to restore, but the old hotels of Miami are worth restoring, too. Only it isn't that easy because they were built fast and cheap in the '30s.

Perhaps they aren't restoring historic hotels so much as finishing the jobs that got started 80 years before. Think of it as the construction equivalent of slow food.

After a day in the windowless conference center, my colleagues and I came out into the perfect late afternoon sunshine and started walking south as evening began to wrap around South Beach.

There's a long stretch of street with one restaurant flowing into another, each one filling the sidewalk with tables making it hard to know where one restaurant ends and another begins. It's like a dream where you're walking through a place that never ends and you can never escape. We walked through block after block of tables of diners, all with pretty girls trying to entice us to eat at their place.

We stopped at a bar where the loud Cuban music made it impossible to talk, but the smooth, complex rhythms flowed through me reminding me of hot nights in the Midwest when I danced to the sounds of the 1930s with the vintage ballroom crowd. I have never understood how people can simply sit and watch a band perform driving dance music, but there was no room to dance, and I probably wouldn't have been able to find a partner anyhow and there's nothing sillier than a white guy dancing the Merengue alone... so we moved on.

Everyone is beautiful in South Beach. The women are almost universally busty, wearing low-cut, short dresses showing leg and cleavage and sexiness. There aren't a lot of dumpy guys, either, which doesn't help me much with my Northwesterner pale skin and soft belly. It's fun to entertain fantasies about the pretty girls, even if they are just fantasies, but harder to entertain those fantasies as they are shattered by the kinds of guys those girls hang off of.

I had changed into a black suit and a dark dress shirt before we headed out because I knew that the clubs in Miami have standards even if I wasn't part of the muscular Latin set. Or maybe especially because I wasn't, and dressing well was the best I could do to try to fit in.

After dinner and drinks our group had dwindled down to me and one of the guys from our group who was in shorts and sandals. I had told him I'd ditch him if there was a dress code, and as he was turned away at the door I did exactly that.

Even after all my travels, I still remember it as the most amazing place I've ever been. I wish I could remember the name, but it's probably in the land of Faerie anyhow.

It started with a room about sixty feet wide that stretched the full depth of the building while the high ceilings made it feel tunnel-like but still spacious. The low lighting came mainly from candelabras and chandeliers that cast soft candlelight on huge, gauzy curtains that created separate spaces that didn't feel isolated from the rest of the club.

There were people dancing to a DJ who was spinning his mix of club music from a perfect little alcove off to the side of the room. Across the hall and by the full-size billiards table, men took turns shooting between sips of whiskey that they had gotten from another alcove with a good sized bar with a marble surface, lit from below, so the effect was a glowing bar and drinks.

The crowd was a mix of young and old, couples and groups and singles, straight and gay, black and white, and every combination imaginable. All well dressed and well behaved. But that wasn't the end of the bar.

As I headed out the doors in the back there was a huge, covered patio with couches and tables with low lamps. People were eating and drinking and talking and there was some light making out in darkened corners. The staff was all dressed in white from head to toe and were quietly and efficiently scurrying around taking care of everyone as the beat of the DJ's music pumped out through a sound system that I never found.

Going deeper took me into a grassy garden where there were more couches and tables with lamps and indoor furniture in the outdoor setting. A big hammock in the middle of the lawn was swaying gently and obviously occupied by more than one person, but I didn't look too deeply to see by whom or how many.

Then I reached the poolside party. Longer than an Olympic pool, the pool was lit from below giving the outdoor space an unearthly quality. The pool was surrounded by couches that looked the size of king-size beds or larger, all filled with the same people as the rest of the place and across the walkway from the lounging groups was a row of cabanas, where people were sitting around tables, playing games, talking and smiling, with more than one bucket with the neck of a champagne bottle poking out of the ice.

And it still went deeper. There was another bar on the back lawn, a sort of Caribbean bungalow with a covered area, and finally a gate that led to a path and out to the beach. I slipped out of the magical party and wandered down to the edge of the low surf where I looked back at the skyline from the low-tide line. The gentle waves of the Caribbean seemed to underscore the mood of the evening -- soft and quiet, obscuring the vast chaos and danger just below the surface.

I returned to my hotel and slept like the dead as my mind tumbled around the schism of my day at a trade show and my night in another world, possibly even another dimension.

The next day I got a call from a client asking if I could get to D.C. the following day to meet with the senator's staff. A quick trip to the kind of gigantic shopping mall Floridians love, buying a white business shirt and a necktie to make my nightclub suit appropriately conservative for the Hill, then a quick change of flights and I was on my way to Washington D.C.

Washington D.C.

THERE ARE FICTIONAL PLACES THAT YOU KNOW INTIMATELY even though it would be impossible to have ever been there. The bridge of the Starship Enterprise is one of those places -- I know the chair, the helm, the science station... I know the thrum of the engines, the sound of the computers.

And I know it's not real. Stepping on board the bridge of the Enterprise is impossible; it's a fictional place that I can see on TV, but a place I know I can never go. My brain would struggle to reconcile what I know to be real and what I know to be fantasy if I found myself aboard the Enterprise.

Which is exactly how it felt the first time I walked onto the National Mall and saw the Washington Monument. It's not a real thing in a real place. It's just something you see on TV. In the distance in one direction was the Lincoln Memorial and in the other direction, Congress.

But it is real. Laying my hand on the limestone surface of the Washington Monument seems almost silly looking back, but at the time I needed that sense of reassurance that this wasn't a dream or a psychotic break, that somehow this place was real.

Somehow travelling to D.C. for business makes it even more real. Looking at the neoclassical architecture with names of government agencies carved into the stone I found myself thinking, "I wonder what it was like in the day?"

Then I remembered, this IS the day -- it's still going on. This isn't just a historical place behind velvet ropes that you look at and leave. The politics, the law making, the history of the United States of America is still being written, and when I'm in D.C. I feel like I'm part of that history.

They call the House of Representatives "The People's House" because anyone can come in. Yes, there are guards and metal detectors, but you don't have to buy a ticket, you don't have to show an invitation, you don't have to sign in, state your business or have your photo taken (although you should assume you're on camera). The congressional office is one of the easiest political buildings to walk into in the world.

But you shouldn't expect to meet your congressperson. They have meetings and phone calls and money to raise.

The Lummi Nation is a small tribe from northwest Washington state. Native tribes still wield enormous power when it comes to getting meetings on the Hill, even if the meetings usually don't lead to anything productive. A tribal chief, with the budget and population of a small-town mayor, can get a meeting with a senator or congressperson with a single phone call and then dominate the meeting for a couple of hours; it's hard for the mayor of Seattle to get a meeting like that.

My unique mix of skills put me in the Lummi delegation, despite my very European ancestry. I got to tag along as a technical expert for meetings in the offices of both senators and congresspeople. It's like getting backstage passes in Vegas; it's not about what they want you to see, it's seeing the gritty mechanics and the all the rigging and lights and hearing the demure leading lady swearing like a sailor because some detail no one else cares about was missed by a stage hand.

The meetings themselves were like meetings anywhere, polite references to promises that won't actually be made, suggestions for how to move forward but with no idea of what direction forward is or what obstacles will be in the way... standard sisyphean politics.

More interesting were the meetings with the bureaucrats. To visit the people whose jobs are secure from election to election is a more involved process. The first stop is in a vestibule formed by a bullet-proof, lucite wall in the lobby where I waited, feeling suddenly unprotected.

As with the People's House, the security screening X-rayed my bag and ran me through a metal detector. Unlike the congressional offices, my ID was checked, my name was logged, and a temporary badge was issued. I then waited for my escort to arrive and accompany me to the floor and room where our meeting was to be.

This may be government by the people for the people, but this is not the People's House.

I'm a tactical kind of guy. Give me a problem and I will work through it to identify the roadblocks and find ways to solve those problems. I believe in open communication to get answers from wherever they may be.

Not surprisingly, Washington does not work this way. Sitting in a conference room with a view of a concrete courtyard and the other wing of the 1960s office block, I was able to find the roadblocks, but not the answers.

"Why can't you just call the Congresswoman and ask her for her opinion?"

"Because that would be a violation of Federal Law."

After the meeting, after being escorted back to the security desk, and after I returned my temporary badge, I stood on the concrete steps outside the building with my colleague where we talked about how to work around the fact that communicating project goals is a felony in American governance.

And that's when I really knew I was in the middle of history. Men in suits on steps of government buildings creating more complex plans to work around already complex situations are part of the backdrop of Washington D.C. just as much as the Washington Monument. They are fixtures that are incredibly important in the right moment of time, and easily ignored when the city becomes just a place where you work and live.

Walking back to my hotel through the Mall and past the White House, I saw a crowd forming for a march. Police were lined up in front of the fence that surrounds the home office of the President, but they were relaxed and chatting with each other so I asked what the protest was about.

"I have no idea," the uniformed cop replied. "There are so many of these I don't even ask anymore."

To the people marching by this was their Historic Day. To the locals in D.C. it was just another day. And there is nothing wrong with that; the squabbles of the day are voiced and the machine of government keeps working.

I was starting to feel more like one of the locals. I had my schedules and meetings and I knew I had to get up in the morning. D.C. is an easy town on foot, with the Metro like a wormhole from neighborhood to neighborhood, and interesting things to see when you come above ground.

You have to be confident when walking through some parts of town -- I was staying in the "U Street Corridor" which is kind of a tendril of low-class cool stretching east of the Dupont Circle neighborhood. As with most tendrils, it gets a thinner the farther you get from the source, until it fades out entirely at the Metro station about 10th Street.

I've never had much trouble beyond some fairly polite panhandling (I accidentally found that if you give them a confused look they just assume you don't speak English) but there are places that I've wandered into and immediately turned around.

There must be some sort of invisible barrier on some of these neighborhoods: one step I'm outside a café with well dressed couples sipping cappuccino and in the next step I find myself watching a drug deal on a doorstep and a homeless guy vomiting in front of me. Step back, sunny cappuccino. Step forward, Quentin Tarantino movie.

Sometimes it's just about what time of year you visit a place. The first time I went to D.C. was in January and I stayed in a boutique hotel in Dupont Circle. Nice little neighborhood, good restaurants, a little artsy. It wasn't until I came back in the spring and saw all the men who had been bundled up in winter were now walking around in tight muscle shirts and holding hands.

The nature of the neighborhood changed for me, even though it had been there all the time.

But you don't have to be in a gay neighborhood to find good food and art.

At what feels like the edge of D.C., somewhere behind the Lincoln Memorial but before Georgetown is the Kennedy Center. The grand waiting area outside the main theaters feels like a modern version of the Great Halls of old castles with incredibly high ceilings and enormous posters draped from the ceiling like heraldic banners that make the large space feel narrow.

Every night before the main performances they hold a free concert and suddenly you realize how big this space is. One end of the hallway becomes a full theater with a stage and rows of seating.

My experience with free government-supported performances has never been what I would call "good." There are a number of adjectives, some of which don't do justice to my desire to rip out my own eyeballs and ears rather than continue to be subjected to something that might actually be an indication of the performer's mental illness. So when my colleague invited me along for the concert, I went cautiously.

The band was described as "a hot new band from Paris whose sound ranges from soft and romantic to energetic swing that shows their Gypsy influences." When they got up and introduced themselves as "The L&O from Paris," the singer, in her heavy French accent, interjected, "from France, not Texas."

And then they went on to play some amazingly good Parisian café music from the era of Django Reinhardt. They were good enough that I bought their CD afterward. I mentioned something about being from Portland and asked them if they had ever heard of Pink Martini; suddenly I was the celebrity simply because I was from the town where their idols were from.

By day there are the free museums to explore. Much of the Smithsonian exhibits are interesting if only because you are seeing the real thing. Visiting the National Archives was interesting, maybe not as amazing and awe inspiring as the first time I walked out onto the National Mall and touched the Washington Monument, but still an amazing place to be.

Of course, the National Archives have a corny exhibit hall with some authentic documents and footage. Teddy Roosevelt spoke from an old film in a high and nasally voice which could have been how he always spoke, or it could have been the technology of the day. As I walked through the exhibits it reminded me of the ride that has replaced touring the Hershey's plant in Pennsylvania -- it's educational, but why travel thousands of miles for something I can watch on YouTube?

But the Rotunda where they display the original documents is history. Dark and reverent, it felt kind of like going to church. They have a range of documents which form the basis of our free society, including an original copy of the Magna Carta kept just outside in the foyer so as not to be confused with our American documents.

The original Declaration of Independence is nearly illegible -- the fading apparently started almost immediately after it was signed. Any image of the Declaration you've seen is a copy of a print made from a hand carved copper plate in 1824. Regardless of how it's holding up over time, that muddy bit of parchment under glass in the Rotunda is still the real deal.

I was also surprised that the Constitution is four large sheets of paper, also fading. I don't know why it surprised me, I've seen pictures in books, but when I imagine the signing of the Constitution it was one sheet of paper, albeit a big sheet. I suppose I get it confused with the Declaration, like any good American with fuzzy history skills.

The glass cases are filled with inert gas and, like in the movie *National Treasure*, the cases are on conveyors that drop into sealed vaults every night. Not that you can tell that in the dimly lit Rotunda -- the display isn't about how the documents are stored, it's about being in the presence of documents that based governance on the will of the people, not an infallible deity wearing a crown.

And history continues to be written outside the walls of the museums.

My timing for Obama's first inauguration was off by one week, but at least it was the week before so I could see the preparations as opposed to the cleanup. If I had planned on getting a place to stay the week of the Inaugural Event, I would have been hard pressed to find anything.

The locals were fleeing the city before the hoopla, and renting their apartments out at a daily rate comparable to their monthly payments. Traditional hotels were packed, and the city was bracing itself for the flood of visitors as if it was a hurricane moving up the coast and for which they could only prepare so much.

There were a few more police-escorted caravans of limos and vans than normal, and conversations overheard seemed to be about what a mess it was going to be during the week of the inauguration, but the week I was there was still business as usual.

Just another week in D.C.

The National Mall had become a walled garden, with the wall formed by every porta-potty from a 200-mile radius. Like a lego wall of giant plastic blocks, they lined either side of the mall with occasional breaks where people could still get through. It had to be one of the most effective blockades I have ever seen -- no one would want to get stuck in the moat of toilet chemicals and human waste.

On the edge of the Mall I saw a small corral of temporary chain-link fencing covered in canvas. The spindly forest of towers sprouting from the vans made me think it was the press pool setting up for the big day, but I noticed the logos were for AT&T and Verizon.

We live in a social world, at least online, and they were preparing for 1.8 million people to text, tweet, share, like and otherwise send out photos of Obama's first moments as President of the United States of America. Even a city as dense as D.C. doesn't have enough cell towers to support that kind of burst of OMGs and LOLs, so they bring in the extra capacity.

When it's finally time for me to leave D.C. I just step on the Metro line and take the train to National. I still can't call it "Reagan," a quirk that probably tags my place in time and politics as much as anything. But even if I don't like the name, I like the airport. Small. Easy to navigate. Easy to get in and out of.

Sure, they finished the line to Dulles and you can take the train there, too, but it takes an hour and a half. National feels like you're still in D.C., just on a commute. When I flew in from Miami, I left my bags at the airport, walked out and used my Metro ticket from the last time I had been there. I was the ultimate infiltrator, the guy who looked like he belonged there.

Of course, I had to come back early to get my bags before checking in for my flight out the same day. I apologized for leaving my bags behind without telling them, but they were understanding enough, certainly not the worst thing they must see in the baggage claim of the nation's capitol.

Then I had a couple of hours to kill before my flight. I re-checked my bags, got through security, fired up my laptop and made calls while ignoring the bustle and noise of the airport. And when I looked up, my flight was gone.

It's one of those incredible sinking feelings like being the last kid on the playground, or getting on the wrong school bus. Lost and alone with no hope of getting home. If I had been a girl, I would have cried; hell, I almost did anyway.

The gate agent was nice enough about it, although he didn't have a lot of pity for me. He understands the timelessness of the airport, how hours pass and the ebb and flow of people comes and goes, but the airport remains the same. He did mention that he had called my name. Twice. But I was too lost in my calls and data to notice.

He booked me onto the 6 a.m. flight, at no extra charge, gave me a number to call which got me a room discount, which was still seventy bucks, and told me where to find the free shuttle. All of which was far nicer than I probably deserved. When I called Markie to let her know I wasn't going to be home until the next day I got the appropriate level of pity, something along the lines of "You idiot!"

I waited outside for about twenty minutes in the D.C. cold until the shuttle finally showed up. The Old Town Radisson shares a shuttle with the Holiday Inn down the street, and it was a very different class of people than I had seen the day before at the Catalina in South Beach. They looked like a rough, prison crowd, grizzled mechanics and transient workers who move from airport to airport and keep the underbelly of the system working.

For some reason the driver had chosen to play heavy choral music on the van's speakers. It was the ominous music movie-makers choose to set the mood as the hero descends into hell with no hope of return. Sitting in a dark minibus, heading to an unknown destination, not at my choosing but from my own stupidity, I found myself in a perfect room in hell.

I got to the hotel, checked in and found myself on the top floor with an incredible view of the city laid out below. It was a nice, basic, hotel room although it had the stale smell of cigarette smoke, which shouldn't be a surprise in Virginia. Then I tried to figure out what I was going to do with myself for the next 10 hours.

I wasn't hungry, but I was definitely too revved up to go to bed at seven (even having gotten up at four in the morning). The front desk had given me a map of the area with some restaurants. Picking almost at random, I headed out towards an Irish Pub.

The clean, quaint, streets of Alexandria surprised me. I remembered a story about how the police in D.C. had herded all the hookers one night across the bridge into Virginia -- I had assumed Alexandria would be similar to downtown Detroit. Turns out it's kind of touristy, with a number of nice restaurants dotting the side streets.

Looking up into a well-lit space, I saw a group of people milling around in what looked like a dance studio. It turned out to be a drop-in ballroom class, to which I dropped in. I spent the next couple hours remembering the Merengue and the Cha Cha, and filling the gender gap as there are always more women than men at ballroom classes.

Dancing for a couple of hours was far better for me than drinking for a couple of hours. Rather than sitting in a pool of my own adrenaline and frustration at some bar, I found companionship and danced away the frustration of missing my flight.

I left plenty of time to catch my flight the next morning, which turned out to be a good thing. My bags had flown on ahead without me and as the TSA agent scanned my ticket, he pulled out a big red pen and scrawled SSS on the bottom. When I asked what that was, he told me it was a selective screening. When I then asked, "Think that's because I missed my flight last night?" he responded, "Probably" in a tone that meant, "Of course it does, you idiot."

So after visiting congressional offices and passing the security of the bureaucratic offices, I got one last pat down as I left Washington D.C.

Just another day in history.

Living in Americana

The truck wouldn't start. I was somewhere in Iowa or Indiana or Illinois... one of those flat states that start with an I, and we still had to reach Cincinnati before the truck could give up entirely.

A friendly voice came over my shoulder, "Need some help?" He wore the standard workingman's uniform with jeans, button-up work shirt and a ballcap with a logo I didn't recognize. His sister owned the hotel where I had stayed the night and where my truck had decided to stop working.

I had decided the starter motor was shot and he offered to give me a ride to get a new one. We got in his new, sparkling clean pickup and headed to town. At an intersection a sporty sedan boomed the beat from rap or hip-hop as it pulled up next to us.

My new friend muttered, "Fucking monkeys."

It took me a minute to process it. Monkey = Black People... Ah. Right... Um... Well...

I went to a high school in Sacramento where there were more blacks than whites. There were more Asians than whites, for that matter. We didn't think about it and racism was just something you read about. I didn't realize it was still alive and well.

And I thought to myself, "Where the hell am I moving to?"

A Hundred Miles from Cincinnati

I DISCOVERED THE TURBULENT STORMS OF A CINCINNATI summer when I moved to Ohio -- the gentle rains of California could never have really prepared me for the full force of a Midwestern thunderstorm. In the midafternoon the blue sky begins to darken, and the breeze begins to pick up. Flashes of lightning can be seen in the distance, and the air starts to cool, but not much.

The thunder starts to become audible and as the sky gets darker with the first drops of rain, the streetlights come on. Soon the flashes are accompanied by a sound like the sky is being ripped apart, and the rain comes pouring down. It gets so thick I can hardly see across the street.

It becomes a chaotic, exciting place with the ripping sound of the wind in the trees, the rain pelting down on the ground, the water rolling off the cement... The smell of wet earth, wet plants, wet rock... The shock of the purple-white light as lightning fractures the sky with blinding spears while the deep resonance of thunder rocks through the house and my body.

Just when I think the rain can't get louder, the wind is almost drowned out by the clatter of hail tearing through the thick maple leaves and bouncing off the cement like tiny ping-pong balls. The hail forms in piles as the rainwater cuts channels in the ice and debris making it hard to tell what is ice and what are flower petals ripped from their stalks.

Then the rain begins to slack off. The thunder and lightning become less and less frequent. Soon, the flashes are silent in the distance again and you can hear the sound of water pooling as it flows from the rooftops and trees. The birds begin to chirp in the lifting gloom and as the sun comes out the smells of ripped vegetation waft through the air and the hail begins to steam and melt as if it had never been there.

Soon it is just another hot, humid, summer day.

Walking in the heat of a Midwestern summer takes a special, slow gait. Like walking waist-deep in water, there is a resistance to moving through the hot, humid air that makes rushing impossible.

It is hard to argue with the logic of sitting on a porch drinking lemonade and whiling away the summer day and then staying on that porch as evening gathers. The fireflies come out with the same slowness as the people drifting in the darkness with that eerie glow.

I learned to dance in Cincinnati summers. Contra dancing is a fast social dance, based on the genteel Country dances of England and France, but amped up with fiddles and banjos in the Appalachia. You have a partner, but you dance with the entire line, working your way up and down the hall, dancing with everyone else.

And everyone else is just as hot and covered in sweat as you are.

Dancing in the summer heat creates an unusual sweat hazard where trying to hold onto my partner's hand as I spin her causes her to shoot out of my grip like a watermelon pip squeezed between my fingers. Everyone is slippery, everyone is hot, but everyone is having a wonderful time.

Summer dances underscore the difference between the sensuality of women versus men. As a woman dances and gets sweaty she slowly sheds articles of clothing becoming more alluring as she glows with the heat of the dance and exposes more skin. A man just gets sweatier and more disheveled as the night goes on, removing his button-up shirt to expose a dated T-shirt design and eventually switching from long pants to shorts that show hairy, knobby legs.

I'm pretty sure men get the better end of this deal and I'm happy to accept a smiling, glowing woman breathing heavily in my arms as we dance and ignore my own shortcomings as a sweaty male.

These are community dances -- the band plays partially for tips but mainly for the chance to play for a room of sober people who can tell the difference between 4/4, 3/4 and even 5/4 music. There are new dancers who have never walked in rhythm, and there are experienced dancers who help the new dancers along. Although there was the time an experienced dancer grabbed me and said, "Come dance with me, I'm tired of missionary work!"

I asked, "Does that mean you're tired of teaching dance or tired of being flat on your back?"

"Both."

And the dances go on. The patterns are woven by men in T-shirts and women in colorful summer dresses as the jigs and reels flow together in dervish-like buzz-swings and sashays.

When I was a kid my father would play John Hartford albums. I had plenty of other exposure to bluegrass music, but in my mind, John Hartford will always be the true voice of bluegrass. After making it big with *Gentle on my Mind*, he decided he didn't really want to be part of the commercial music world and he went back to his roots of steamships and cotton.

Dancing in Cincinnati to the Appalachian style of Contra dance tied dancing to bluegrass, bluegrass is tied in my mind to John Hartford, and John Hartford's bluegrass is tied to steam powered paddle wheelers.

One hot summer morning under the sound of the steam calliope I boarded *The Belle of Louisville* for a dance on the Ohio River and I thought of John Hartford's song about *The Julia Belle Swain:*

> *Oh the Julia Belle Swain is a mighty fine boat*
> *She's a mighty hard boat to beat*
> *She raced the Belle of Louisville*
> *She beat the Delta Queen*

And here I was, on the boat that beat the *Julia Belle Swain*.

Louisville is a big, modern city, but as bluegrass songs all tell you, the river runs muddy and the river runs wide. The sternwheel began to turn and push us away from shore and away from the 20th century.

The dining deck had been cleared out for the dancers with the band at the front, right up near the bow of the boat, playing jigs and reels with their backs to the view as the *Belle* paddled her way up the Ohio river.

As much as it felt like the 19th century, the band was amplified. But even with the speakers helping the music waft over the crowd, there was the other, more driving rhythm of the steam engine turning the big sternwheel.

If you were lucky enough to start the dance near the top of the hall, you would be dancing to the music. If you started at the end of the hall, you danced to the {*whoosh*}-[*chunk*], {*whoosh*}-[*chunk*], {*whoosh*}-[*chunk*] of the piston driving the boat up the river.

Somewhere near midship there was confusion as the two rhythms overlapped, and we moved from dancing to the music to dancing to the steam engine or vise versa. Not that it mattered. We were dancing on the river on the deck of an old steam powered sternwheeler on a hot summer day, and that was all that mattered.

Louisville was about a hundred miles away from Cincinnati and it seemed every city was about a hundred miles away. I could drive to Louisville or Indianapolis, or Lexington and it was always a little less than a couple of hours -- just far enough to be an adventure, but not so far to be a trek.

I overshot Lexington the first time I drove there. The main freeway loops around the main city and I realized the signs stopped mentioning Lexington and said I was on my way to Richmond.

The gas station attendant had a thick Kentucky drawl and when I asked him I how to get to Lexington as he slowly said, "Well.... yuh can't git there from here." Then he laughed and gave me clear driving directions back up the road and the right exit to take.

This is a state that keeps the Bureau of Alcohol, Tobacco and Firearms in business; this is bourbon country (although Makers Mark is in a dry county and you can't actually taste it at the distillery). And it's tobacco country.

Having lunch in a steakhouse in Lexington I noticed a reader board on the wall. It would go through a cycle of trivia questions and drink specials, and then remind me that I was in Kentucky.

> *Smoke*
> *{blnk}*
> *Smoke*
> *{blink}*
> *Smoke {start sliding to the left}*
> *...Anywhere you want to in this establishment.*

Not only was there no non-smoking section, they were actively encouraging me to light up at the table or at the bar or in the can or by the hostess station... Smoking, it seemed, was not only a right, but it was encouraged the way fans encourage you to wear team colors. It's not just something you do, it's important to the community that you participate.

Surprisingly it was on a trip north to Columbus, Ohio where I saw the big Confederate flag painted on the roof of a barn. I expected Kentucky to be, well, "Suhthern" but despite sharing a border with Kentucky, Ohio should be Northern. Borders are not quite as precise in the real world as they are on maps.

Driving through Columbus late one night I came around the corner and saw Jesus. A statue inside a church was backlit, creating a giant silhouette on the three-story windows of the back of the church. I'm sure many drivers shouted the Lord's name the way I did, and I wonder how many might have crashed in a moment of terrified prostration.

Cincinnati is a Catholic town, with St Xavier University and a number of large Catholic churches. It may be that influence that makes the town feel less "Southern" but it's definitely a conservative town with companies like Proctor & Gamble and Kroger dominating the business world. Suit jobs in 90 degrees and 90 percent humidity are not fun, but it's that kind of town. The air-conditioned offices are required, but the slam of heat as I stepped outside in the summer probably took years off my life.

Eventually the oppressive humidity of summer slacked off and was slowly replaced by dry cold air. Snow in Cincinnati just sticks around, never really melting, never really getting any better. It slowly gathers a sheen of grey from the exhaust and dirt wafting from cars, fireplaces, grease fryers and the city itself. The buildings and cars get that same grimy buildup -- there is no sense in cleaning windows or washing cars in the cold, dirty winter.

There is no color to the world. Parks are filled with bare lifeless trees with grey snow and an increasing number of muddy tracks where people crossed the spaces that were lawns in the summer. Roses and vines are cut back and even if they aren't their leaves shrivel and disappear with the stalks soon to follow.

As the city turns grey and dirty so do the people. My lips would get chapped in the cold dry air and I bundled up in grey dark clothes to try to stay warm in the wind, snow and ice. I stopped noticing that the scarf I wrapped around my face every day began to reek of sweat and breath. I learned not to touch my car without gloves, the way a child learns not to play with a candle from putting her hand in a flame.

I hid from the winter by parking in garages and moving through the city by way of the Sky Bridge network that connects buildings above the street, like some early version of the City of Tomorrow; unlike the city of the future with pedways forty stories in the sky, the covered walkways in Cincinnati connect the second floor of one building to another, and I walked through corporate lobbies, shopping mezzanines and sometimes a hallway of locked doors like through a tunnel bored into the canyon walls of the city.

One day, I would realize I felt good for no reason. The ice had quietly melted and the air was warmer with just enough humidity that it didn't hurt to breathe and I found myself walking outside without an environmental suit. The earth was still bare with plants just below the surface and the trees had just the slightest protrusions of green buds. Then a bird sang and the symphony of spring exploded on my senses.

Mild California never prepared me for the joy of spring. Art and poetry about the season has spilled forth for millennia. To me, spring was just a little nicer than winter and not quite as warm as summer. But in places like Cincinnati where they have real seasons, spring is like a release from prison, shackles thrown aside, to find that you not only love the world, but it loves you.

The Not So Deep South

SHE WAS A FLORIDA NATIVE, SOMETHING I DIDN'T KNOW existed, and she had Southern charms. A friend of a friend suggested she show me around Orlando because I kept complaining about how there was *nothing* in Orlando.

I needed a local to show me around because up until this trip I had been staying where my client booked me, usually in some family-oriented hotel near Disney World. I had tried to explain to him that it's just weird for a single man to stay where children played in the pool way into the drinking hour and where breakfast included Mickey Mouse waffles.

There is a "local Orlando" but it's hard to find as it is being steadily overwhelmed by The Mouse and people who are looking for a generic American lifestyle -- they don't actually want to be in Florida, they want to be in an idealized world that never existed, and somehow manage to miss the irony of building family communities on alligator infested swampland.

My client's gothic McMansion was in a gated community on a golf course. He didn't understand when I laughed out loud when I saw the house was on Valhalla Drive... Berserkers swimming in a private pool after a day on the greens isn't what I had pictured, and probably not what Vikings pictured either, as they died in battle.

He was in one of three golf developments which were all adjacent to one another. Homeowners were sorted depending on their financial and social status. He wasn't in the one where Shaq and Tiger had houses, but he wasn't in the cheapest community, either.

Sitting by his pool in the screened-in lanai that kept the mass of bugs at bay, I could hear a {*clack*}{*clack*}{*clack*}{*clack*}{*clack*} of baby alligators snapping at each other and anything else that moved in the golf water hazard that doubled as a decorative pond by the house. The phrase "middle class luxury" rolled through my mind as I tried to figure out what bothered me about the scene.

Other than its enormous size, other than the stone entryway that was worthy of the street name outside, it was just another suburban home. I like to think that if I had a couple million dollars to spend on a home I wouldn't just do a bigger version of what I have now. I would want more variety; they chose more of the same.

But that seems to be the theme of themes in Orlando. Build a bigger Disneyland with bigger versions of the original. And build enormous homes in enormous gated communities that are just bigger versions of LA suburbs.

Toward the end of my trips to Orlando I started booking my own travel and discovered there was actually a city, not just a sprawling mass of shopping centers, subdivisions and theme parks. Downtown Orlando feels like a Midwestern town, even if it's in the middle of Florida. It has tall buildings of steel and glass that aren't quite tall enough to be called skyscrapers, one-way streets with too many cars, and people rushing to and from important things.

When I checked into the boutique hotel in downtown Orlando I discovered that my friend's friend and local guide for the night had sweet-talked the front desk. As I entered the room I found a book called *Touring Central Florida*. She seemed intent to prove Central Florida wasn't just The Mouse and swampland.

We met for dinner at her small house not far from the central downtown. The neighborhood reminded me of Palo Alto with stucco bungalows from the '20s and '30s along narrow tree-lined streets. The artificial small town of Celebration that Disney built like some *Twilight Zone* community doesn't have the cracks in the sidewalks or the garbage cans blocking driveways like this part of downtown Orlando that Disney is trying to imitate, and it doesn't have the soul of the real neighborhood either.

Dinner was at a restaurant on a quiet side street downtown... walking distance to my hotel, again discovering something I didn't know people in Florida did. Walking, that is.

It was wintertime, so it was in the seventies with no bugs. We sat outside on a patio space but eventually had to move inside because she was cold; at first I thought she was joking, it was such a perfect night, but I forget that people who live so close to the tropics think that seventy degrees is "a bit chilly."

The next day I drove up to Winter Park. My book told me that the towns in Central Florida were so close together because the US Army placed forts at a day's march from each other, otherwise the troops would be slaughtered at night by the Seminole Indians. Eventually the settlers overwhelmed the natives by sheer numbers and the towns grew up where the forts had been.

It was hard to picture the carnage of warriors fighting to the death in Winter Park. Here is the old Florida, a retreat from New York in the late 1800s. There was an art fair in the town square, a real town square with real art, not a Disney town square with stuff from China. I got a sandwich on a baguette and an iced coffee and sat on a patio facing the square, feeling like I should have been wearing a white linen suit.

As I crossed a canal, crowded with vegetation and overhung by trees with Spanish moss, I understood the original draw to this part of the world. Warm winters with beautiful lakes and room to spread out with gardens and lawns.

The Orlando area of today is an imitation of the splendor of the Central Florida of that brief history in time between the war with Seminoles and the surrender to the Mouse, but there are still pockets of the dream of the 1890s if you take time to look. And it only took me two years to find it...

In the north end of Florida there is a place that reminds me of a TV show from the late sixties where humans from Earth found themselves on a planet of giants. Even though the humans were in a city of the giants, every outdoor scene seemed to be in a nondescript jungle with occasional bits of building or other artifacts sitting incongruously in the foliage.

That's how I remember Jacksonville, Florida.

There doesn't seem to be any urban planning, or any planning at all in Jacksonville. The road goes along through tall trees and thick brush and there's an auto-repair shop. More trees and greenery, and there's a hospital. There are places where the buildings get denser and the vegetation thinner, and then reverses again a short distance down the road.

At one point a body of water opened up to one side of the road and in the distance across the water I saw what looked like a downtown area, and then the trees and bushes closed in again and I was lost in the jungle once more.

A lot of Florida is like this -- loose zoning laws allowing people to do pretty much whatever they want wherever they are. There is a little bit of the Southern git-er-done attitude, but a lot of the building and business in this part of the world comes from the urban developers in the North who have gotten tired of government telling them they can't put a tire-disposal yard next to a housing development.

In Jacksonville you don't have to worry about the ugliness next to your house because there isn't anything next to your house. Just trees and swampland.

I was in Jacksonville for a conference that involved a lot of law enforcement. I declined the demonstration of the background check software, knowing the things on my record that might actually pop up probably wouldn't help my company's position any.

I sat with the Nikon sales team in the bar drinking on their tab. We had started around two in the afternoon. People came and went and I lost track of how many drinks I had had. At around six or seven in the evening, the strippers showed up with their DJ who seemed to only have a bass machine and no music, and I suddenly realized how drunk I was.

It was one of those learning experiences that some of us never really learn from. Don't drink yourself to the point of throwing up until there's nothing left, ever. And definitely don't do it when you're at a professional conference and you have to get up in the morning and talk coherently about physics and computers.

Probably the only good thing that came out of my trip to Jacksonville was learning that Alka-Seltzer actually works wonders for a hangover. Hardly the best review of a destination, and not a place I ever want to go back to -- both the place and the hangover.

Jacksonville isn't really a place, anyhow. And it certainly isn't the South even if it is right on the border with Georgia. Ironically, to visit the South I have to go further north.

Atlanta is a big place. It feels even bigger when you're stuck in traffic, which is most of the time, but unlike Jacksonville, it's not just spread out, it's a dense city, too.

I was getting coffee in Midtown Atlanta one morning thinking about how all the streets seem to be named Peachtree, when I saw the Portland Timbers sticker on a laptop. I almost did a double take; this wasn't just any soccer club, but the Hipster's soccer club in Portland.

The owner of the laptop had recently moved from Portland to Atlanta for work, and while he missed the Northwest he said he liked living in a town where he could drive. Portland has a way of judging you harshly for a big car, where Atlanta gives you points. He liked that he could buy a house, and he had found people who liked soccer, brewed beer and ate good food.

During my stay in Midtown Atlanta I found the hipster food that I had been promised. Grilled trout from a local lake, a sweet potato mash that wasn't overly sweet and steamed vegetables with just enough seasoning to let you taste the actual vegetables.

And then there were some amazing cocktails that I wish I had written down.

Like I said, Atlanta is a big place. Even though strip malls and chain stores and subdivisions dominate most of Atlanta, it's so big it can support a hipster ecology in the cracks between the southern sprawl.

The Home Depot is based here, and the joke I made about working with their tech team was they are not only what we in the Internet business call a "brick-and-mortar" company, they actually SELL bricks and mortar. So I shouldn't have been surprised by their sprawling headquarters in a gigantic building on the edge of Atlanta.

The two towers are only 19 stories high each, but the building is almost a mile long, with the wings of the building crawling up the sides of the towers to form something that looks almost like a kid's Lego project. The enormous corridor through the ground floor is always filled with people in orange aprons; employees get points for wearing the apron even when they work in the white-collar office.

When I went for lunch in the cafeteria I was reminded that this is, indeed, still the South. Most of the basic American foods were represented -- the hamburger bar, the pizza bar, the sandwich bar... There was something called the Spa Bar, which served what passed for healthy food, usually pan fried chicken or a grilled pork chop with a salad.

Everything was served in styrofoam clamshells and I picked up my plastic bag with the plastic fork, knife and spoon while trying to balance the smallest cup I could find, which was 16 ounces. The only iced tea was sweet tea, a kind of tea that has so much sugar in it that if you add any more you will see crystals forming around the sugar you just added as it pulls the sugar out of the supersaturated solution that sweet tea is.

It's trips like these that make me glad I don't have any of the dietary restrictions everyone seems to have these days. If I was gluten intolerant, or vegetarian, or worse yet, vegan, I probably would have starved that close to Marietta.

But when in Georgia, sometimes it's just better to get the pork chop and gravy and a big cup of sweet tea.

Vegas, Baby!

LAS VEGAS IS THE COMPLETE OPPOSITE OF MIDWESTERN America and the South. Where steam powered sternwheelers still ply the Ohio River, there is nothing historic or traditional on the Vegas Strip. But there is no way to really talk about "Americana" and not talk about Las Vegas because it is as uniquely American as those sternwheelers.

The same scrubby rocky country that runs along Interstate-80 four hundred miles to the north surrounds the glitzy city of sin. There is a range of mountains circling Vegas to the north which makes me think of the Shield Wall on the planet Arrakis in *Dune* -- those mountains kept out the storms and the sandworms to form a habitable patch on a deadly world. The mountains in Vegas are probably serving the opposite, keeping the sprawl from killing the desert.

It took me two or three visits to Las Vegas to actually go to what you would call Las Vegas. I had a client who ran auto repair shops and he asked me to tour the shops around Vegas. I budgeted about five hundred bucks for air and hotel, and got a bundled deal for a first-class ticket and a third-class hotel room for $400 -- I figured two hours each way in first class trumps less than eight hours sleeping in a hotel room.

So I stayed in the old downtown at the Lucky Horseshoe, eating a sandwich and watching a science documentary in my room, hiding from the cigarette smoke and incessant noise of the gaming machines.

During the day I toured the auto shops, riding in the client's flashy Dodge Viper convertible with the top down. The city of Las Vegas itself feels like a Southern California town with quiet subdivisions, supermarkets and parks, and children going to school. Like living near Disneyland, the Vegas Strip is always there, but it's not the center of life if you're raising a family.

In Orlando or Anaheim, Disney is hidden away. But in Las Vegas, the Strip is always visible over the rooftops and supermarkets. The tall buildings are clustered together forming a massive single object like some alien mothership sitting in the middle of a conquered human community, reminding you that they are not going away.

Lunch with the client was in a buffet in a small casino in North Vegas. The massive amounts of roasted meat and chilled seafood and every dessert imaginable are subsidized by the constant ringing of slots and other gaming machines around the perimeter. While not the Las Vegas Strip by any means, it is still Vegas, and a machine is always ready to give you odds and take your money.

Toward the end of the day I found myself in a Home Depot. The utter normalcy of The Home Depot was the exact opposite of normal. I found it almost jarring to be in a place so familiar after the desert sun in the convertible with the Strip brooding on the horizon while recovering from the casino buffet. We walked in, I scanned the aisles to orient myself and I led the way to the ethernet cable.

Walking back out to the car I discovered that a box of cable doesn't fit in the tiny space left in the trunk of a Dodge Viper when the top is down. I stood by the car as the hydraulics lifted and moved panels around like a Transformer, transforming it from a car with no trunk into a car with a top, and just enough trunk space for the box.

At the end of the day I returned to my hotel room, got a few hours' sleep and slipped out in the dead hours of the early morning to catch an early flight. Having seen the actual town, but not the Strip, I left early enough to visit the core of the mothership while the aliens slept. I drove down the broad street in the warm desert air at four in the morning and slipped into the enormous, and disturbingly quiet, parking structure at the Bellagio.

The Strip at four in the morning is a sight few people have seen. I say this with confidence because there were almost no people on the streets, and even fewer on the walkways.

I walked through the Bellagio's broad carpeted promenade, hearing the electronic come-hithers of the lonely gaming machines. In the distance there was a card game that could have come out of a Rat Pack movie -- men in white dress shirts with open collars, jackets dropped on the back of the chairs, more than one guy standing and shouting about whatever had just been played.

Crossing the bridge from the Bellagio to Bally's I found a 24-hour Starbucks with the most beautiful woman I had ever seen waiting for her order. Short cocktail dress, perfect stockings, perfect hair and makeup with beautiful eyes and a friendly smile. Her order came up, and her tray came out and I realized she was a cocktail waitress, cast for the role as much as hired.

As daylight started to touch the sky, runners in designer gear started to emerge from the hotels into the warm desert morning signaling the end of the night in Vegas and the start of a new day. I got back in my car, and headed back to the grey weather of the Northwest in February.

A few years later I was sitting in a cabana by the pool at the Hard Rock Cafe. As I sipped my gin and tonic, I chatted with guys from Rackspace about what kind of hosting options they had. It seems there is always a bit of business in everything in Vegas.

I was in town for the Clio Awards in 2010. Every night for three nights there was a different set of awards, with increasingly more recognizable hosts. I was there for my work on the *Mad Men on Twitter* campaign as I had been putting Roger Sterling's voice into 140 characters or less; it had turned out to be surprisingly easy for me to channel the jaded, skirt-chasing, heavy-drinking ad man from the 1960s.

Matt Weiner was in the casino that night after getting a special award one night for creating *Mad Men* and bringing a romaticized agency world to the masses. My friend and Twitter collaborator, Helen, grabbed me and dragged me over to meet the man known for the absolute control that made Mad Men an amazing bit of television. And here I was, some schmuck who had completely co-opted one of his characters.

He and his wife were trying to slip out of the casino as we caught up with them. He was relaxed and in a good mood, graciously accepting my apologies for putting words in his character's mouth, saying he really liked what we had done and appreciated the challenges of tweeting from 1963.

All the while I'm thinking, "This guy created *The Sopranos*, too, didn't he?" But I never did get a bullet to the back of the head, which I take as a high compliment.

After a few more drinks and a little dancing in the Hard Rock, I headed back to the cruise ship of the desert, the MGM Grand Hotel. In typical fashion for me, but atypical for Vegas, I walked the mile and a half between the hotels. Housekeepers and other people in nondescript uniforms were the only other people walking and they quizzically watched the man walking in Vegas in jacket and slacks, probably wondering what bet I had lost.

The backs of the casinos on the main Strip towered in front of me as I walked from the Hard Rock to the MGM. The roar of six lanes of street traffic and the glare of the headlights were almost relaxing after spending too much time in the too-dry air of casinos with the smells of stale cigarette smoke and scented air freshener. The flashing lights and constant bombardment of the electronic tones from the gaming machines had been jarring me at every turn while the blackjack dealers looked my way with the come-hither of well-dressed carnies.

Vegas is the exact opposite of what I look for in a vacation -- I want something relaxing and away from the distractions of our modern world. Casinos are designed to steal money from people who like shiny objects and can't do math. They are filled with lights and smoke and loud drunk people, a far cry from library books on the wrap-around porch of a Pennsylvania inn.

But the other reason to travel is to go somewhere to learn new things and experience something truly unique. And if you want to experience America, you have to visit Vegas.

The Strip is so American it's almost a parody of America. I say "almost" because it *is* what America does best. The science and technology in this place is astounding; the fact incredible technology has been exploited to create a giant, corporate complex that jacks up visitors like some kind of consumerist crack whore is just part of what we do in this country.

Vegas pushes the boundaries in all directions at once -- extreme engineering with more hotel rooms on the corner of Las Vegas Boulevard and Flamingo Road than in all of San Francisco. The acquisition of masterpieces from Masters such as Monet and Da Vinci is almost overshadowed by the amazing collection of contemporary artists with their private galleries.

Sure, Donnie and Marie are doing a show tonight, but there are also three Cirque du Soleil shows. Every celebrity chef has a massive restaurant here, and while we're spoiled with amazing food carts in Portland, one of the best meals I've ever had was at an Emeril's, of all places.

Look past the giant TVs, the blaring advertising, the enormous buildings, the hawkers on the sidewalks, the strippers-to-your-room billboards towed by large trucks down the middle of the street… Look past all these things and you see the industrious, dreaming, driven part of America that put us on the Moon.

It's the part of America that constantly innovates and makes something new out of thin air, solving complex problems for fun and profit. While it's garish and wasteful and opportunistic, if you live in this country you live with this evil twin of the industrious, innovative American in a wheat field you see in political campaign commercials. And those commercials of wheat fields and family values are made by the Vegas Americans.

I'm not suggesting you embrace Vegas; not everyone needs a *Hangover* weekend. But I do suggest you look at the marvels that make this scar in the desert also a miracle in the desert. We are all flawed creatures, but we are also amazing creatures -- Las Vegas amplifies both sides of our American values and our American debauchery.

So while Vegas is buried deep on my list of places I want to be, I can't help but enjoy myself while I dig into concentrated America -- because America, good or bad, is an amazing place and so is Las Vegas.

Oregon

I was walking along the canal in Chester, about 20 miles south of Liverpool where I met a young couple with a stroller. When they heard my accent they asked where I was from.

"Portland, Oregon."

The young mother practically swooned as she said, "Oh... Portland! We really want to visit there."

"Really? How do you even know about Portland?"

"We watch Portlandia.*"*

To be honest, we could have a worse ambassador than the quirky show that pokes fun at the town that likes to say about itself, "Keep Portland Weird." Any time I try to defend Portland from a sketch like the one with the angry bicyclist, or the drivers who refuse to go first through an intersection ("No, you go!") I find can't argue...

Yeah... it's pretty much a documentary.

The Other Portland

IN SEPTEMBER THE EMPTY-NESTER TOURISTS COME TO THE Pacific Northwest. They are looking for a quiet place to spend their retirement, away from the noise and dirt and crime of the cities where they made their livings. The weather is perfect, the air not just clean but full of oxygen from the lush forests and the rich Pacific Ocean. Some of them can't resist the pull and come to stay.

Then the rain begins.

In October it comes and goes. Big clouds push across a brilliant blue sky, merge together, and rain comes pouring down. Then holes form in the clouds, and the sun comes out, reflecting from the dripping wet world like off a giant multifaceted mirror.

The rain complicates many of the very things people move to the Northwest for. Bicycling in 38 degree rain is not fun, especially when you share the road with spray from the four-wheel-drive monsters people tend to choose for our long winters. The autumn leaves are beautiful, until the rain turns them into a mush that looks remarkably like Corn Flakes left too long in the milk.

Then November comes. The days grow shorter, the clouds grow thicker and the sun breaks become less frequent. As November turns to December the cloud cover becomes an almost permanent ceiling over the world.The sun doesn't really rise so much as the sky gets lighter around eight in the morning, and then darkens again around four thirty. For many people this is when the depression starts to set in and the "For Sale" signs go up.

I personally like the dim days and the long season of cool wet weather. The days and evenings roll together like some gothic twilight; I prefer to keep the lighting low in the house having installed dimmer switches on every light so it feels more like candlelight than 21st century lighting. Going into fluorescently lit office buildings is as jarring as the lights coming up in the bar at the end of the night, and I try to avoid either situation.

Portland has an anachronistic feeling of a timber or fishing town from a forgotten past in part because our weather makes us seek out places where we actually want to hang out. When you're going to hide from the rain in a public place for a few hours, you don't have the patience to sit in an Applebee's or Red Robin. You need to feel like you're at a private club in the 1800s.

Our cozy pubs are cozier in the winter. The wood smoke from our local pub calls me in from the street, and the random musician in the corner keeps me around for the third pint as much as the prospect of going back out into the rain for a cold, wet walk home. And during the day, our coffee shops are like a warm blanket with that jolt of caffeine that makes it possible to get back into the fray.

Every now and then I have one of those quintessential Portland evenings. It almost always involves alcohol, and some combination of quirks that you just don't really expect to find outside of a Hunter S. Thompson novel. But, then, Portland might actually be a Hunter S. Thompson novel, and I just have yet to discover that quirk.

I went downtown to meet my buddy Don; Don's a commercial electrician, born and raised in Oregon. What he lacks in hipster skills, he makes up for with that blue-collar aloofness that I think is what hipsters are really trying (and failing) to pull off. We were sipping strong ales by a big, open garage door at the Hair of the Dog Brewery in the old warehouse district on the east side of the river. Don told me to look at the building across the street.

Up on the second floor were huge, old windows that opened into a photography studio. It was obvious they weren't doing school portraits. Even at that vantage point I could see she had perfect hair, perfect make-up and perfect everything else. If the tight dress left little to the imagination, the pulling it off seductively for the camera removed any need for imagination.

I mentioned this to the guy sitting on the other side of me and we got into a conversation about the quirks of Portland. Turned out he was a senior editor for the scientific journal Nature and was in town for a conference for the Scientific Committee on Antarctic Research. The acronym seemed appropriate for beer and strippers.

So we chatted about peer reviewed science while glancing up at the studio windows from time to time the way men in other bars glance at the football game. It was just something to look at between swigging strong beer and eating a collection of locally cured meats.

As he was on a quest for decent beer, I felt it was important to drag him to Apex bar where they have fifty-odd beers on tap and not a Budweiser in sight. The place was packed with the usual assortment of bizarre Portland styles of furry faces to '80s hair to spandex to piercings and to T-shirts with Linux command lines (the one with the command for "file system consistency check" being particularly amusing).

Apex might be packed because you can bring in the great Mexican food from Los Gorditos next door, or maybe it's the huge bike parking area, or perhaps the seating for a small army of beer drinkers at the outdoor tables. I don't really know, but the fact they had Old Rasputin on nitro was just icing on the cake.

A stop across the street at BeerMongers found us one of the only two kegs of a wood-aged Saison brewed that year -- there had been some kind of event the night before where brewers brought out some of their really special stuff, but then it seems in Portland that there's always some kind of really amazing brewing event.

And that's the quintessential Portland bit -- there's always this amazing rare brew, a beautiful woman nonchalantly taking her clothes off in public, an intellectual twist like an editor of a science journal checking out the bar scene and it's all just another day in the town I choose to call home.

Of course "Portland" isn't just one thing. There are little neighborhoods like hippie Hawthorne or the urban Pearl District. There's the poor, but gentrifying, North Portland where realtors forced all the black families to buy or rent back when it was legal to be a racist. There's the West Hills where the wealthy white people still live because it's still financially feasible to be a closet racist.

But most people agree there are two main parts of Portland. The city is divided east and west by the Willamette River. The culture most people think of as "Portland" is an eastside thing -- the food carts, dive bars with good music, coffee shops where baristas can create the Mona Lisa in the foam of your tiny latte are all on the east side of town. The west side is known for chain restaurants, rolling subdivisions and people who work for a living.

I like to think of Portland as a brain -- the west side, or the left side, is where the managers and business people live practical lives with white-collar jobs that require process management. Meanwhile, the east side, or the right side of the brain, is where the artists and creative class of people live.

Think of the river as the great longitudinal fissure between the hemispheres of the brain and the bridges over the river acting as the corpus callosum -- the bit of the brain that connects the two hemispheres. People cross the river on the bridges, going east for funky art and west for jobs in cubicles. The river, like the longitudinal fissure, is largely ignored.

After 20 years of not noticing the river I found myself with a boat. It wasn't my idea and every man I tell that it was the woman in my life who talked me into buying a boat thinks I'm trying to shift the blame for owning a boat the way a drug addict says, "I was just holding it for a friend!"

My experiences on the water before the boat included an adventure when I was a kid and my dad lost control of a sailboat in the San Francisco Bay. The sail hung slack and flapping uselessly while he tried to start the auxiliary engine and we kids were all sure we were going to be dragged out to sea (apparently we weren't anywhere near the Golden Gate, but that's how I remembered it).

There was also the family friend with a power boat. He was one of those middle-aged guys who never matured enough to have friends his age and, instead, surrounded himself with teenage boys which led to uncomfortable, inappropriate events that are still tied up with boat ownership in my mind.

Markie, however, had owned a boat before with her late husband. She grew up in Oregon and her childhood memories included going fishing with her dad on the lakes and rivers of the Cascades, so her baggage was lightly packed with happy memories while I was carrying a steamer trunk on board our boat purchase.

But we had a friend who was getting rid of a boat at a ridiculously cheap price. It was a twenty-year-old, 18-foot, open-bow Bluewater -- big enough to take some friends out on the river, but small enough to be manageable. I figured if I hated it we could easily sell it and get our money back.

I didn't hate it.

Cruising through Portland on the Willamette River is like finding an entirely new world in the middle of the city. Like slipping into Diagon Alley, there are only certain places where you can cross from Portland to the world of the river. But when you do enter this world, you find a stretch of countryside, nearly 27 miles long, with ever-changing landscapes, all in the middle of the city.

The mouth of the river, where the Willamette meets the Columbia, feels almost like going out to sea. The barges and giant container ships from Asia create wakes that turn into rolling waves that crash into each other and chop the river into a dangerous, chaotic death trap for a little boat like ours. I've sat in the outflow of the Willamette watching the waves but I've never dared leave the comparatively calm waters of the mouth of the river.

On the east shore of the Willamette is Kelley Point Park where people come to play in the water and drink as much beer as they can carry in with their large coolers. Although Kelley Point is an open space, it edges up to industrial land and office parks. Across the river, the west shore is the open farmland of Sauvie Island where Portlanders go for U-pick berries in the summer and corn mazes and pumpkins in the fall.

Cruising up the river with industry on the left and farmland on the right, there is little resemblance to either the eastside funkiness or westside money of Portland. Soon the towering gothic spires of the St Johns Bridge come into view. There's a small dock and boat ramp at Cathedral Park, not named for a nearby church but for the arches under the bridge that tower over the park like an old European church.

The next bit of river is even more industrial than the last. Huge drydocked ships being worked on at the shipyards on the east shore and warehouses from the Port of Portland resting on pillars over the river on the west side creating deep, dark spaces that look like flooded Egyptian tombs. The river between the port and the shipyards is wide and usually fairly empty of other boat traffic until you reach the northern edge of downtown.

I-405 races overhead with peregrine falcons nesting in the girders high up in the arch of the giant Fremont Bridge. North of the bridge is a rail yard and the Port of Portland, but as you pass the bridge the Port warehouses are replaced with waterfront condos. The east side of the river is still a bit rough and weedy, but you can see the sports center and light rail rolling along Interstate Boulevard, giving an urban touch to the shoreline.

Then comes the Steel Bridge, with its heavy black girders looking like they came from the Industrial Revolution with giant rivets holding the whole thing together. Sitting in the boat under the bridge I can be directly under a freight train, which is in turn directly under the main deck with cars, buses and light rail. And at certain times of year, the bridge is under the flight path of the Portland Airport. A plane above a bus above a train above a boat floating in the river.

The seawall on the downtown side of the river is a sheer cement barrier with no ladders and no way out -- if the boat sinks on the west side of the river I would have to swim to the east shore to clamber out. On the top of the wall I can often hear music festivals and smell the cooking of food carts that service the various beer fests and other events, but from the surface of the river, it's like a medieval fortress with no way in.

Soon the wall disappears and there is a large grassy area, often filled with people and music. And just beyond that, floating in the river, is a mediocre restaurant that has gotten more mediocre as it has changed hands from the local conglomerate to a regional conglomerate. But nothing can ruin the joy of pulling up in the boat, tying off right next to the restaurant, and getting beer and fish and chips while sitting outside on the dock.

The trick with an old boat is to avoid the embarrassment of killing the engine right beside the people enjoying their outdoor dinners. When it is time to leave, I untie from the dock, hit the engine and get out quickly to minimize the smell of gasoline and exhaust, and head farther upriver with the throttle wide open.

Almost immediately I push the throttle back down as the Willamette passes under the tall, utilitarian Marquam Bridge, with cars jockeying for position on I-5 overhead. The Maquam is followed quickly by the Tilikum Crossing, the new bridge made famous for allowing every form of transportation *except* cars, then under the simple lower arch of the flat-topped Ross Island Bridge where the river changes again.

I have a choice at this point in the river, up the west side of Ross Island, where I can fire up the engine and whip along the river at full throttle with the office blocks and condos on one side and a nondescript shoreline covered in a forest of maple trees on the other. Or I can take the slow route, the no-wake channel between Ross Island and the east shore.

I prefer the slow channel. It's hard to believe that a stone's throw away are the tall buildings and seawall of downtown because this section of river makes me feel like I'm out on some Midwestern tributary to the Mississippi. Tall trees on either side, slow quiet water, and gentle turns where you might see deer on the shore or eagles flying overhead.

In the middle of Ross Island is a giant lagoon, made larger over the last 90 years as the local cement company mined it for gravel. In the summertime there seems to be an endless party of young people with their boats tied together on the north end of the lagoon. Music blares from the enormous speakers of whichever boat is hosting the party at the moment. Girls in tiny bikinis lounge on the bows of the boats and boys either try to chat up the girls or yell at each other while drinking massive amounts of cheap beer.

The older folks tend to find spots on the south end of the lagoon, spaced out sufficiently to give a sense of privacy as if at a resort on a mountain lake. Occasionally someone jumps off the side of a boat with an audible splash and then a shout as they find the water is still a bit chilly. Of course the shout is always followed up with, "No, it's fine, you should get in!"

There are large barges anchored here and there, waiting to provide fresh gravel to the Ross Island Sand and Gravel Company that no longer mines the lagoon for their namesake product. They still mix concrete on the east shore of the river but the rusting girders and shacks of the old mining operation sit abandoned on the island.

Just over the tops of the trees you can see the towers of the South Waterfront development -- glass and steel condos peering into our wilderness retreat like a futuristic city built on the edge of a post-apocalyptic world that's starting to recover.

Leaving the lagoon, I'm careful to take it slowly through the no-wake zone in the channel on the east side where paddleboards and kayaks abound. Silently cruising by on the eastern shore are the scores of bicycles on the Springwater trail, some for fun, some for serious exercise, but for many it's just an easy way to get downtown from Sellwood.

The north end of the channel opens to the houseboats at the Willamette Yacht Club. The houses are a mix of nice to amazing. From time to time I'll see one of the houseboats on the cover of a design or lifestyle magazine like *Sunset*, always taken from an angle that doesn't quite show how closely packed together the floating homes are. Slips can cost up to half a million dollars, and that doesn't include the houseboat itself. But it still feels like a trailer park for rich people to me.

The owners of the floating homes in the self-proclaimed yacht club reach their community by way of the amusement park. Floating on the river, I can hear the screams of the roller coaster or the toot of the steam whistle from the miniature train ride at Oaks Park and catch the occasional whiff of grease from the fryers.

The Sellwood Bridge is really the southernmost part of Portland proper but the greater Metro area continues, and the river changes again. I don't know if it's because of the depth or the fact it's sheltered by the hill on the west, but south of the Sellwood bridge the water gets calmer, at times it takes on an almost glass-like quality. Perhaps it's in respect for the dead that fill Riverview Cemetery on the quiet western hillside.

Soon the expansive golf greens of Waverly Country Club come into view with perfectly manicured lawns that roll down to the shoreline. Waverly is an extremely exclusive club with rules and rituals from years gone by. On a summer evening the patio is filled with wealthy families putting in their required dining time at the clubhouse, socializing as membership requires. The clubhouse itself always reminds me of that resort in *Dirty Dancing* -- rich, isolated people in a perfect setting ignoring the gritty world outside.

And that gritty world is just next door as I take the boat around the wide bend of the river at Milwaukie. The golf club on the east side of the river disappears and is replaced with the downtown area of Milwaukie's roaring main drag with gas stations and mini-marts.

On the other side of the river are the grand houses of the Dunthorpe neighborhood. Still technically part of the city of Portland, these rambling estates with private docks and houses that can be truly called mansions, form a community that doesn't seem part of the city I know and I only find my way to it by the river, making me think it's part of a pocket universe in the river and not really part of the rest of the world.

The river continues to change as we go further upstream. It's wilder in some ways, with a sheer cliff across from Elk Rock Island; an island that stops being an island in the summer when the water level drops enough that the locals walk out to the rocky beaches to swim, sun themselves and slip off into the bushes for some adult time.

The jetskis start to show up as we cruise past Lake Oswego. There are nice houses all along the river on the east side with small, private docks where they store their boats and toys, making it easy to have a casual party on the dock while everyone takes turns on the jetskis.

As I pilot gently up the river with my passengers lounging with champagne or beer, I'm constantly trying to find a course that will keep me clear of the speedy little watercraft. Of course, the times that I'm in more of a hurry and running full throttle, they flock to my wake like seagulls following a fishing boat, jumping and flying off the waves my boat leaves behind.

There is respite from the speedboats and jetskis at Hog Island, really more of a big rocky chunk of land in the river. The main channel goes east of the island, but I nose the boat up the smaller channel on the west, throw anchor and swim in the deep cool water in the shade of the tall trees and steep hill of the west bank.

As we near Oregon City the river changes once again. It broadens to a wide, shallow playground with even more jetskis and speedboats. There are a couple of big sandy beaches lined with pickup trucks and cars.

The farther we get into Clackamas County, the more we see the real Oregon -- blue collar redneck Oregonians. Tailgaters in the eastside of Portland are hipster foodie events with fancy wines and hoppy beers. Tailgate parties on the river in Clackamas County are hot dogs and chips and cheap beer without a hint of irony.

The river changes one more time at the far end of Oregon City, far more dramatically than any turn so far. The entire river rises up 40 feet above us at Willamette Falls, the entire flow of the river pours across the 1,500 foot arc of rocky cliff churning the river water all around the boat. Natives have fished for eel in the falls probably as long as the falls have been there. But while it is a great natural formation, the area is anything but natural.

Along either side of the river are old industrial buildings of dull sheet metal and concrete. Channels and sloughs were cut or built to use the power of the river in the days we relied on gravity to power our industry, but the water all comes back together in the narrow channel below the falls.

The water tugs at the boat, sometimes pushing us downstream, sometimes grabbing the hull and turning the boat in unexpected directions. Old wires or metal structures still hang over the river and I get a sense of unease sitting in the water.

Between the sound of the roaring falls, the lack of control of the boat in the current, and the harsh, aging industrial compound it feels like an Arnold Schwarzenegger film where an alien monster is hiding in the shadows, slowly picking off the humans, and maybe the dog.

This is as far up the river as I can go without putting the boat on a trailer and taking it to Wilsonville. You can still see the locks that lifted boats up to the river above, and gently lowered them back down, but the state closed the locks in 2011 so our way is blocked.

It's actually amazing they kept the locks open that far into the 21st century. After all, there's the line from the old song that sums it up perfectly:

> *Oh the railroad trains, the bus, and the planes*
> *are taking up all the slack*
> *He's been watching all those river towns*
> *slowly turn their back*

But there's another line from a different John Hartford song:

> *Oh the river run wide, run deep, run muddy*
> *The river run long after I am gone*

And I'm sure it will.

Bicycling the Cascades

MY BROTHER AND I RODE OVER THE SELLWOOD BRIDGE EARLY on a Saturday morning in June. The back of my bicycle was loaded with panniers filled with camp gear and piled with my sleeping bag and tent. Clamped to the forks on the front were two more bags stuffed with more food, clothing and gear.

The plan was to ride for two weeks to Lake Tahoe from Portland -- after climbing mountains for two weeks, we would be in perfect shape for the 130 mile, 15,000 foot climb over five passes in a ride aptly called the "Markleeville Death Ride." Just drop the packs and racks and relearn how to ride with a higher center of gravity, already acclimated to altitude and hardened for the climbs.

And so the two of us headed through Southeast Portland and towards the Cascades. Portland itself is a very bicycle-friendly town, but you quickly leave Portland as you enter Clackamas County. We found ourselves on a busy road, negotiating storm drains and debris in the shoulder that wasn't really wide enough to be considered a bike lane.

Then the city thinned and we started up the winding road to Estacada. While there was less traffic out on the country roads, the shoulders were non-existent. Pickup trucks hauling boats and cars going too quickly around the corners put our lives at risk at every turn. And we were doing this for fun.

Estacada is one of those towns that if you blink, you miss. Unless you're on a bicycle. The two lanes in either direction make the town feel like a big city after winding along the river through pastureland. We stopped for lunch before heading out of civilization and into the Mount Hood National Forest.

The roadside campground deep in the national forest was a place where people go to get away from it all but bring all their stuff. Tucked around the campground were trailers and awnings with camp lights that can probably be seen from space. Music from competing stereo systems floated through the air as the campers slowly erased portions of their memory with massive amounts of beer and liquor.

But when you've ridden over 70 miles with full packs and it's dark, it's easy to ignore the noise of people communing with their version of nature and fall sound asleep.

The campground was dead silent at dawn as we ate a cold breakfast and struck camp, putting tents and sleeping bags back on tiny bicycle racks. I had two pairs of bike shorts, and the ones I wore the day before were still wet from the vigorous washing I had given them in the camp sink the night before. The trick is to strap it on top of the gear and let the sun and wind do their magic while riding another day.

We rode farther into the Mount Hood forest, frequently checking the map to be sure we didn't end up on a skinny forest service road that looked just like our skinny forest service road only would have led us away from civilization and into the "Tragic Story" segment of the evening news. The route took us slowly over a ridge, and then our heavily laden bikes flew down the other side into the town of Detroit which is nothing like its namesake in Michigan but rather a small community that exists just to feed and fuel the people who boat on the lake or are on their way to some adventure in the Cascades.

It was about 11:30 in the morning when we came into a little roadside cafe called The Cedars -- it's one of those diners that embraces its mountain home with lots of varnished pine, old sawblades mounted to the walls and grainy photos and old art of loggers, trees, and mountains.

They were still serving breakfast but when I ordered the ham and cheese omelet they said they weren't doing omelets anymore. My body was craving the easy protein and fat, but, nope... No omelets.

So I ordered scrambled eggs and asked if they could put some ham and cheese in it, which was no problem. It seemed like an amazingly easy thing that they couldn't think of. Of course, to a waitress there is a huge difference between an omelet and a scramble, but to a bicyclist burning 8,000 calories a day, it's not about the form of the food, just what's in it.

Then our climb began in earnest. Forty miles up the Santiam Highway with a steady climb. It was agony every time I reached the top of a rise that took me back down, even a short distance, because I knew I would have to climb back up another hill, and then more.

There were breaks in between the sound of engines and wind from the cars rushing by, and in those breaks I could feel the forest. The warm air rising from the asphalt mixed with the cooler air flowing out of the shadows of the trees with the smell of fir and earth.

At one point a giant snow-covered peak loomed into view above the trees. You can't see Mount Jefferson from the Willamette Valley, so it was surprising to see a peak as big and snowy as Mount Hood that I didn't know existed. Hiding an entire mountain that close to Portland seems like quite a trick, but it reminds me just how big the entire chain of the Cascades is when I think about how big the hills must be between me and the peaks.

Finally we made the last climb up Santiam Pass and crested the summit, passing the marker for the Pacific Crest Trail where people with more adventurous souls than mine backpacked along the spine of the mountains. Our water bottles were all dry so we pulled into Suttle Lake -- I had danced at the camp that was just inside the entrance to the area, although I hadn't remembered it was a Christian camp in the summer.

Two sweaty guys in spandex begging for water at the kitchen door must have been a bit of a sight, but we were able to get water and make the final 20 miles into Sisters where we had planned to camp, but after 120 miles in the saddle, the Best Western was too tempting to pass. The hot water never ran out but I don't think it could completely melt the sweat and road grime.

Early the next day, the bikes fully loaded again, we headed into Bend. You can tell that you're getting into an urban area as the garbage and broken glass start to increase, and the toots of passing cars go from friendly "hellos" to blaring "get off my road!"

We probably spent too much time in Bend that day -- John needed a part for his bike so we had to kill a little time waiting for a bike shop to open, and then we needed to get some food, which turned out to be in an organic co-op with a cute hippie chick dressed for the summer weather with sheer clothes and no bra and who seemed really into the two brothers riding the length of the Cascades.

We eventually pried ourselves from her siren charms and started the next climb out of Bend and up to the top of Mount Bachelor.

We had filled our water bottles and had extra water in the large, collapsible skins of rubberized canvas that we had each bought for just this occasion -- riding for hours into the wilderness on an exposed mountain road with the sun blazing down and reflecting from the road and the rocky hillside.

When you're climbing a mountain on a bicycle you have the constant reminder of how slowly you're going. My speedometer told me I was going something like 5-7 mph, which meant the 20-mile climb would take over two hours.

At some point I got tired of seeing how slowly I was going and how few miles had passed and how many miles were still ahead, so I flipped the digital display down so I would stop obsessing over how hot and tired I was. A few pedal strokes later my curiosity would get to me and I'd flip it up again, only to establish a repeating cycle.

The road surface up to the top of Bachelor is rutted and cracked. All winter long it is subjected to freezing and melting while being driven on by heavy four-wheel-drive vehicles with chains or studs digging into the ice and pavement. But just past the resort is the road leading down into the Cascade Lakes area, and that bit of road is kept closed all winter long.

Passing through the open gate was like leaving hell and entering paradise. The pristine asphalt was smooth and felt almost soft in comparison to the rough road we had climbed up. And it was downhill -- a fast, smooth ride into cooler, moister air with more trees and wildflowers at every turn in the road. South Sister rose above a green mountain meadow as we came towards the end of the hill.

The momentum from the downhill run started to fade and I began to pedal again. Oxygen from the thicker air and growing things filled my lungs and I felt like I could take on the world. On the next hill we discovered a problem with the cooler, wetter air.

Bug season.

It seems that the biting flies and mosquitoes can find you if you're going about nine miles an hour, which, when climbing a hill can take a bit of effort to exceed. And once they find you, you have to get up to about 13 miles an hour to drop them again. An Italian racing coach couldn't be as effective to get me to stand up in the saddle and push my way up the next hill as a million little biting bugs descending on me.

When we got to camp I hurried to get my tent set up. The mosquitoes followed me to the shower, and while the hot water spray kept them at bay, the coin operated shower cut off after three minutes for a dollar. I rushed back to my tent and zipped myself in. As I huddled in the tent with my flashlight I could see the needles of the swarming insects trying to force their way through the netting, hoping to score a drop or two of blood if I got too close.

The next morning came. Eat. Strike camp. Load the bike. Ride.

The Cascades are a volcanic range. At times the road cuts through lava fields with sharp rocks and boulders jumbled around the flat surface where a crew had crushed and cleared the way when the road was built. My brother brushed off his geography degree and lectured about the different kinds of rocks we passed. Which at least let me breathe as I struggled up another mountain.

The road to Crater Lake goes through more lava beds and dry stands of trees that seem so far apart it's hard to call it a forest, but as you climb you can see more of the land around the mountain -- thicker trees to the west, scrubbier and dustier to the east.

Our ride had been taking us back and forth from the lush Pacific side of the range to the dry high desert of Eastern Oregon, and from here we could see both ecosystems with the same plants looking much bigger and healthier on the west side than the east where they starved for water.

We sang *Bohemian Rhapsody* at some point on the climb. I'm sure many people have summited Mount Mazama by bicycle, and many of those have done so with full packs, but I'm guessing very few sang Queen songs on the way up. My apologies to the wildlife.

The dry mountainside didn't change much, the road just leveled out and was still a strip of asphalt cut through lava fields covered in a thin forest. Then there was a turn and the lake peeked into view. And then it disappeared again making me think it wasn't ever really there. We finally came around the last bend and up to the visitor's center and there was no doubt that we had arrived at Crater Lake.

When the mountain blew its top nearly 8,000 years ago, it left a deep caldera. Imagine a deep moon crater about six miles in diameter, but take away the harsh white glare of the surface of the moon and replace it with browns and green where the trees grow on the steep slopes inside the crater. And instead of an ink-black pool of shadow or a glaring white plain in the bottom of the crater there is an expanse of clear blue water.

Now imagine that the water doesn't just sit in the basin, but goes deep -- deep blue water that goes down another half mile. And put it on Earth with clear blue skies and mountain air. And you can imagine why it's so hard for me to describe it.

Of course, that mountain air can be a problem. This wasn't the Moon, but I had used all my oxygen bicycling up to the lake and it turns out there isn't much oxygen at around 7,000 feet. I tried eating but I felt sick. I just wanted to curl up in a ball and pass out.

John told me to get on my bike and we headed down to the campground a couple thousand feet lower. As we sped down the switchbacks on the southern face of the mountain I started to feel better. By the time we got to the campground I was hungry and raring to go; unfortunately the campground wasn't open yet and the store and restaurant were vacant.

I made do with what I had in my packs, and crawled into my tent to get away from the mosquitoes that had come back with the lower altitude.

Get up. Eat. Pack up. Ride...

This is the problem with setting hundred-plus mile days. You have to ride constantly. With full packs and stopping to eat and use the bushes it's a ten-hour day of bicycling. Then camp, then sleep, then another day of riding. At some point it starts to feel like a job.

So I bailed on the Sierras and the Markleeville Death Ride. We rode the comparatively shorter ride into Klamath Falls with the lake on one side and a cliff wrapped in chain link on the other -- sometimes falling rock really does mean falling rock.

Klamath Falls itself is the center of the agricultural area in Southern Oregon, and it also has a small college, The Oregon Institute of Technology (not nearly as well-known as that school in Cambridge). I think a college immediately makes any town much better to visit. We found a funky vegetarian restaurant with crazy art on the walls and in the morning I got one of the best lattes I had had for what seemed like a very long time.

John continued alone down the ridge of the Sierra Nevadas, and I put my bike on the train heading north. The four days riding south took ten hours by train, and I got home in time for dinner, albeit very tired from days of riding and a little tipsy from a day in the bar car...

Michael R. Bissell | 98

The Dry Side

IT WAS PERFECT WEATHER IN THE DRY AIR OF CANYON CITY. MY dad had turned off the highway at John Day to visit an old ham radio buddy who had retired there from California. We were sitting on his patio, high up the hill, sipping lemonade and dancing around the politics of Portland versus the rest of Oregon.

Our conservative host seemed to drop a non sequitur into the conversation. "I'm all for the reintroduction of wolves!"

Taking the bait I asked, "Really?"

"Sure! Just start in the Park Blocks in Portland. If they want 'em so bad, they can be the first to have 'em."

I imagined a pack of 100-pound wolves skulking through the trees of the Park Blocks past the Portland Art Museum and jumping into action, knocking over the bistro tables outside the espresso bars while chasing a pink-sweater-clad shih tzu.

He had a really good point.

Oregon is really two states -- the "Portlandia" Oregon is the I-5 corridor with Portland and the college towns of Eugene and Corvallis dominating the politics of the state. In the green Willamette Valley we make laws that ban hunting cougars with dogs, or protect wolves as they come back into Oregon.

But the bulk of the land in the state is on the other side of the Cascades, in the sparsely populated high desert... the dry side. They don't take vacations to see wolves and cougars in the wild, the wolves and cougars come to them. They worry about their children being attacked when they see the bones of a kill on their property, and they work hard for very little money, and have to deal with the loss of income when they lose livestock.

This is real cowboy country, where ranching and wheat are the core of the economy, along with some mining, timber and not much else. Along the north edge of Oregon you travel through places like Pendleton, home of the Pendleton Roundup rodeo and the wool company known for its lumberjack shirts and horse blankets, that proudly bears the city's name.

Ruts carved by wagons that traveled the Oregon trail are still baked into the hard earth running through the hills. I-84 is pretty much on the original route of the trail -- the trail became a track, the track became a road, the road became a US Highway and the US Highway became an Interstate Freeway. It's all the same dirt the settlers fought their way across although some of it has been graded and paved.

The scratches in the desert were just the beginning of the scars settlers have left on the land. In the Elkhorn Range of the Blue Mountains is a place where the earth has been torn to shreds by a landlocked boat. The Sumpter Valley Dredge sat in a small pond of its own making, chewing up the ground looking for gold. As it dug forward it pushed gravel behind, slowly moving its tiny pond around the valley, leaving a trail of destruction behind.

The mighty Columbia River has been dammed, and dammed again, creating water for agriculture and electricity for the entire West Coast. The aluminium smelters came to the Columbia because of the cheap electricity, but today it's the giant server farms of Google and Amazon living on the power of the Columbia.

On the ridges for mile after mile are the giant white towers of the wind turbines. From the air you see them lined up far into the high desert, looking like the crosses in the Arlington Cemetery, giant white stake followed by giant white stake in a massive grid pattern. From the road they look like some kind of alien invasion standing impossibly tall on the horizon, waiting for orders from their masters.

Earlier in the road trip with my dad we spent a night in the Geiser Grand Hotel in Baker City, a bit east of Pendleton. The high-ceilinged rooms with dark wood and an amazing stained glass canopy that you look up at in the dining room and down on from the central stairs must have been beyond opulent when it was built in the late 1800s. Whether you arrived by wagon or rail or on foot or horseback, after hundreds of miles of empty, dusty country, the hotel must have felt like heaven.

It's still nice, but Victorian luxury pales a bit after suites in Las Vegas and resorts in Florida.

The city itself has become another nondescript collection of concrete buildings. The view out our window faced the majestic Wallowa Mountains, but all you really noticed was the parking lot with the bright white glare of high-pressure mercury streetlights and the large RV parking area. Of course, it could have been a smelly stockyard in the past for all I know.

My dad made some joke about it being the Geezer hotel, and as a geezer, he wandered off to bed while I went to find the hotel bar. I sat in the quiet bar that slowly got less quiet. Turns out there's a big transient population of twenty somethings working the restaurants and hotels where urbanites come to stay on their way to and from horse packing and camping in the Wallowa mountains to the north.

The night had that young, Portland vibe because the tourists bring their money and their ideas of what service a quaint town should have. The Old West bar at the Geiser has an espresso machine and I was able to introduce a young woman to an espresso martini.

She didn't like it.

It turns out the hip, foodie culture with young people trying to find new experiences is a thin veneer laid on top of the Far West culture. Most of the people in the bar were from the middle of nowhere Oregon. Baker City is *Bright Lights Big City* to them, even though you can blast past it on I-84 without realizing you've missed it. It's a cosmopolitan cow town, but it's still a cow town.

To see a real Eastern Oregon town, go a couple hundred miles south to Burns. Harney County is bigger than the entire state of New Hampshire, but with one half of one percent of the population. Burns, with only 2,000 people, has almost a third of the county's population.

After miles of sagebrush and rock, you know you're coming into town by the slow increase of sheet metal barns and two-wheeled tracks in the gravel leading off the side of the road. The billboards for truck maintenance, real estate and motels start to show up, the road becomes four lanes, and you're still not quite in town.

The thing is, the town never really gets going. There is a main drag with some old brick buildings, but nothing over two stories. The whole town seems spread thinly as if the people who live in this part of the world are trying to avoid each other. Or maybe they are just trying to fill up a city as best they can with few people.

Farther south is horse country -- wild mustangs run through the Steens Mountains, descendants of horses escaped from Spanish explorers hundreds of years ago. Finding them is harder than you might think; they have taken on a dusty color through the generations that disappears into the dusty hills.

Standing on the top of the Steens looking down the gorge to the north with binoculars, I kept thinking I saw a wild horse, only to look closer and see it was a cow. I don't really know why a wild horse is more majestic than a wandering cow; they both live off the dry grasses in the mountains of Southern Oregon, but one is living a dream, and the other is just chewing its cud.

A storm was blowing through the Steens the day I drove up from Frenchglen. The mountains aren't what you normally think of as "mountains" but rather a chunk of earth that's been shoved up like when a block of sidewalk is lifted up from its neighbor. It's a slow, steady drive up a gentle grade, and then a 5,000 foot drop to the Alvord Desert floor.

The rain that had been overhead down in Frenchglen became wet fog halfway up the climb. Then it fell off the cliff. It looked as if you could walk off the side of the mountain into a giant field of white and grey cotton candy that was turning to pink and gold as the sun set behind me.

When the weather cleared the next day, the sheer height of the cliff was still hard to fathom. The Alvord Desert basin is a featureless plain covered in a thin layer of salt from a long-since dried up lake. In the distance you can almost see mountains, but the plain seems to go on forever.

Whether filled with clouds or dry and empty, it feels like standing at the edge of the world.

There really isn't much more out there -- one day driving in the far southeast corner of the state I was stopped by a flagger. They were repaving the road and I had to wait for the pilot truck to come back through and lead me through the construction. When I asked him how many cars he had seen that day, he looked over his notes, did some mental math and replied, "Four." I was the first car he'd seen in about an hour.

There are more cliffs like the Steens tucked away in Southern Oregon, some even have turnouts marked as a "Hang Gliding Zone," not that I saw any people gliding overhead.

In fact I didn't see many people at all, or animals, other than a surprised burro foraging on the side of the road. I was driving the cartoon car that day, and I always think the burro looked up to see a bright blue streak with a superhero cartoon and said, "What the heck is THAT thing?"

I'm sure he wandered a bit farther from the road after that, getting away from the craziness and fading into the silence of the big country that is Oregon.

California

The horse was rental, the kind of horse that is resigned to walking the same trail week after week with a different person-shaped sack of potatoes on his back. I had helped take care of horses in Sacramento and ridden some; at least I didn't embarrass myself mounting but I can't say the horse's opinion of me was particularly high.

The trail to the meadow and our campsite wound along creeks and through trees and into rocky fields. A line of horses with a mix of riders slowly spread out as we climbed higher. As I came around the bend in the trail I heard the distinct shaking noise of a rattlesnake.

I had seen Bonanza, *I knew what was supposed to happen. The horse was supposed to panic, rearing up and either tossing me on the rocks or running blindly off a cliff with me hanging from the stirrups. The horse had not watched as much TV as me -- it looked at the snake, turned to the left, walked around the coiled, rattling serpent, and we continued on our way.*

The North Coast

THE BUS FOR REDDING LEFT SACRAMENTO AT THREE IN THE morning and immediately got on the freeway that it would stay on for the next three hours. I-5 is a boring drive in the daylight and I've heard the road engineers made it zig and zag up the valley to keep drivers awake by forcing them to turn the wheel from time to time.

There was nothing to see but the occasional lights from a town as the express bus rolled along in the dark of night. It pulled into Redding as the world went from dark to the dull brownish color of morning twilight reflecting from the dull brownish landscape of the valley as it ends and the Siskiyous begin.

There was an isolated world of activity at the bus station as people bustled around collecting or loading luggage, meeting or saying goodbye to friends and family, but the silence from the town beyond was almost tangible by contrast. Redding is a sleepy town on the weekend, and the world outside Redding was empty and quiet.

I was able to get a cup of coffee and some sort of dough that had been fried and glazed in sugar, and then I caught the Redwood Empire Lines bus to Arcata. The road from Redding to the coast starts out straight and smooth as it heads out of town and past Whiskeytown Lake, but soon it gets steep and winding, showing its logging road roots.

The bus struggled up the hills, and my stomach kept trying to get up and move to another seat each time we went around a corner. The one or two times we were at a stop for more than five minutes I had to get out just to steady myself and then it was back into the nausea compartment. Eventually the bus arrived in Arcata and I sucked in lungfuls of coastal air which helped to push the road-sick, stale air from my body.

The other way to get to Arcata is to fly. The Arcata airport (which is in McKinleyville) was built by the Air Force in World War II to test fog penetration equipment for fighting the Blitz in London. It's one of the foggiest places on earth, so you can expect your flight to be delayed, and if it isn't delayed, it's going to be bumpy coming into a place bordered by the grey Pacific ocean on one side and the steep Coast Range on the other and where the rain never seems to stop.

I had moved to Arcata to attend Humboldt State, which was as far as I could get from Sacramento and still pay in-state tuition. I just didn't realize how isolated that far away could be.

Arcata is like a little enclave of the hippie days of UC Berkeley grafted onto the North Coast. Like a family from the 1950s living in a bomb shelter who have kept Cold War culture alive, Arcata has a new generation of hippies who don't realize the world is very different outside their remote hideaway.

Still, it is some of the most beautiful country in the world, at least to my eyes. Not everyone can handle the constant rain but without that rain you wouldn't have the emerald green fields that the Irish say look so much like home.

Of course there is that sauerkraut smell in the air from the pulp mill across the bay from Eureka and the highway is a bit dodgy with the logging trucks, but get off the path and there are the beaches in Trinidad to the north, the forest behind the university in Arcata, and the rolling hills where sheep and cattle graze and cheese is made down by Ferndale in the south.

When I lived in Arcata I would drive or ride my bike out to the Mad River Beach and hike the mile or two up the beach to the mouth of the river. I had no idea it was right next to the airport, with their light schedule I never heard or saw a plane gliding over my campfire in the dead of night. I would smoke my pipe and talk to the ocean knowing that I was completely removed from any human creation.

The south end of the Arcata/Eureka area is bordered by the Eel River Valley; I still have a print from a painting that depicts a spotted owl with its kill in a tree -- the political nature of the painting escaped me when I found it in a gallery in Ferndale and instead I saw the depth of the forest and the river and the ocean beyond.

Old growth forests still stand south of Fortuna in the Avenue of the Giants. New York can have its Avenue of the Americas (even though they don't want it); the twenty to thirty-story tall trees crowding the road are far more interesting towers than the skyscrapers of Manhattan.

On a foggy January evening deep in the redwoods along the old highway I found a little set of summer cabins. After promising not to use the kitchen, I was able to get a cabin for the night at half the regular rate -- any business is good business in the dark season on the Avenue of the Giants.

I sat in the knotty pine paneled cabin, read a bit, and enjoyed a bottle of Spaten Optimator I had found in the back of the small market. The teenaged cashier said he had never seen it when I complimented the store's selection. He guessed the owner bought it more for himself than any of the locals who come in to buy cases of Bud and Coors.

This is a part of the world that I would love to live in except for the people. When I was in college I had lived with a girl from Myers Flat -- years later I cruised through the small settlement to see if it was the same as when I was in college. It was. While I love the idea of living in the foggy redwoods near the sea, the reality is one of poverty and inertia that keeps people stuck in the mud of Humboldt County.

Of course, there is one cash crop. I had been warned not to hike in the Forest Service lands because there were trip wires tied to shotgun stakes -- think of a rainbird on your lawn only instead of spraying water, there is a nozzle that holds a shotgun shell and sprays a blast of iron pellets.

The tripwires weren't for people, but for the deer that love to nibble the buds as much as people love to smoke them. Growers told me that if they didn't keep the deer out they could find an entire crop devastated in a couple of days by a single herd.

In the eighties President Reagan had declared the War on Drugs and military helicopters flown by Vietnam vets cruised overhead looking for camo netting that hid large crops. In my short career selling imprinted T-shirts we would sell shirts with a picture of a fistful of marijuana buds emblazoned with *This Bud's For You* or with cartoons of what looked like a war zone with helicopters raining fire down on fields of pot. The growers and the enforcement teams both bought them in steady numbers.

The War on Drugs destroyed what was left of any economy in southern Humboldt County in the eighties. Corporate raiders had come in and bought the logging companies, cut whatever they could and shut things down when they couldn't squeeze any more blood from the hills and the people. I would see spindly logs stacked up in the mills; maybe they could get a couple of two-by-fours out of the young trees, but most of it went into chip board or the pulp mill in Eureka.

Of course, things have changed again. When I went through Garberville recently there were plenty of new cars on the street and restaurants and specialty shops line the main drag. The helicopters are gone and the Cash Crop is back.

California Highway 1 begins, or ends depending on which way you come from, at Leggett. US-101 continues down the valley and winds its way through Ukiah and Santa Rosa, but to get to the California coast you have to go over the ridge.

My brother John told me about the time he drove an old panel truck down from Eureka to Fort Bragg. The brakes and the gearbox weren't what you would call "reliable" and he headed down to Willits and Highway 20 rather than tumbling off a cliff while risking Highway 1. But even Highway 20 is a tough road in a big truck with little control -- the hills are like a garrison wall keeping the idle masses from overwhelming the quiet coast.

I have driven over the ridge from Leggett to Fort Bragg more than once, getting car sick even in the driver's seat. I rode over it on my bicycle once, slowly grinding up the steep road, and braking steadily down the other side, because even on two wheels, the 10 mph corners are hard to take any faster without dragging your panniers on the ground.

The Pacific Ocean finally comes into view between two hills where the road slips into a small river valley that shrinks to almost a canyon where the road leads out to the ocean. A dairy barn sits clearly on the inland side of the last hill, facing out to sea like a guard post just inside old city walls.

Then the road turns to parallel the shoreline, cutting along a thin slice in the earth in the steep hillside that towers above and falls down below, making me feel like I was driving on the edge of the Earth, although I don't know if it's because the land ends at the ocean or the ocean ends at the land.

This is the southern end of the Lost Coast -- you can't really get there from here, without going back over the hill to Leggett and traveling north to Garberville and then taking the road out to the coast again. There you will find the rolling hills with sheep and cattle. It's where the water starts to change from the Mediterranean blue of the south to the silver and dark grey waters of the north.

The air is fresh, scrubbed by the ocean and forests and meadows, and hardly touched by the hydrocarbons we live with in the real world. There are no coffeeshops, no boutiques, no extra-dry martinis. Just the wind and the rain and the sun and the world.

But I'm on Highway 1. I can't head north and the highway takes me farther south away from the hidden country of the Lost Coast. And suddenly I find myself in Fort Bragg.

Fort Bragg is a good place to get gas, but it isn't part of the awe-inspiring beauty of the North Coast by any stretch of the imagination. With a long, straight section of city road divided by a left turn lane, the town rolls along for a few miles with old buildings that haven't gained character over time and newer buildings that were built with the same utilitarian mindset.

The air still has that scent of ocean and forest, but the town makes it more like other places in the world where people commute and garbage is hauled.

However, this is the home of Old Rasputin. I think I might actually enjoy an evening with the crazy Russian, but I'm talking about beer and not just any beer -- Old Rasputin is a flavorful glass of nostalgia for the Pacific coast, served with a Russian-grade portion of alcohol.

There's a dreamy quality to drinking this imperial stout that fits with the days of sunshine and fog on the North Coast. It has a flavor that hits like the tang of smoke from a fire of salty driftwood on the beach and I feel warm and relaxed as it washes over me. Like its namesake, it's crazy, complicated, and it will be the ruin of me... but somehow I don't care.

On a nitrous tap it's another world. The beer is pushed out of the keg, through the lines, into the glass, across my palate and into my belly with smooth, tiny bubbles -- the same gas that keeps you giggling while the dentist pulls your impacted molar.

And so I drink. I drink briefly to the fall of the Tsars. Then, I drink to the sea lions and the crashing surf. I drink to the wild irises and the white-crowned sparrows. I drink my overly strong ale and think about a time that never happened where I lived happily between the woods and the sea.

Farther south the country softens and rolls along bluffs. My nose picks up the smells of my childhood, which I hadn't realized was so heavily scented with eucalyptus in coastal air until driving down the coast on a nostalgia trip, There is a familiar rhythm to the road as it dives inland where a creek has formed a cove, and then back up and out into the sun along the bluffs.

The small towns are quaint and artsy once you leave Fort Bragg behind. There are artists and galleries living off an economy driven by wealthy people who come and stay for a while and then go away. The gritty underbelly is hidden away in the hills in small houses and trailers where the people who work for the transient wealthy try to get by for another day where money is tight, but the thought of leaving is unbearable.

The ocean is decidedly different this far south, bluer and warmer, even with the north wind that constantly blows, pushing the tops of the waves higher until they form into whitecaps dotting the ocean.

And then my nostalgia trip pulled into a deep part of my childhood as I reached the Gualala River at the end of Mendocino County.

The Sea Ranch

IT WAS SUMMER SOMETIME IN THE 1970s; MY BROTHERS AND I were sitting in a sauna at the "Big Pool" at The Sea Ranch on the northern Californian coast when suddenly one of us said, "What the hell are we doing?" We had escaped the oven of the Sacramento Valley just to bake in a wooden box by the ocean...

With rolling meadows above the bluffs and forested hills, The Sea Ranch spreads along nine miles of California Coast at the very northern edge of Sonoma County; not quite Mendocino, too far north to be part of the Bay Area and too coastal to be part of wine country. It was our hidden country, and as a kid I always imagined Narnia looked a lot like The Sea Ranch.

My grandmother built a house at The Sea Ranch in 1969, back when it was more of an "artist's refuge" than the rich person's getaway it later became -- we knew trouble was coming when the cops started driving Volvos and booting cars.

For years I had a recurring dream where I went back to visit The Sea Ranch only to find minimarts and subdivisions. And while it has grown with more houses and a golf course and it feels more like an HOA than an artist's community, it is still a special bit of coastline.

The unpainted wood siding of the houses with unique open architecture supported by large, flat roofs propped up on one end create sharp angles on the rooflines with vaulted spaces inside. The master plan for the community tried to keep parking hidden from the road and nestle houses in the landscape to make it feel more like Ecotopia than a planned housing development.

One day I came across a large black and white print in IKEA with the distinctive weathered wooden fence line and trees above the crashing Pacific of the Sonoma coast. Even though I stood under the industrial fluorescent light in the crowded Scandinavian store, I was home, in a grove of Mendocino Cypress trees, feeling the steady north wind that bent the trees in the same direction and smelling the mix of sea and meadow and woods that is burned into my memory.

When I was seven or eight I scaled a cliff like the one in the photo and when I got halfway up I discovered what sandstone means as the rock began to crumble in my hands and under my feet. I kept scrambling because it was easier to see a path up than back down and barely made it to the top, inches from a tumbling death.

I visited that beach recently and even though it turns out the cliffs are about half as tall as I remember from when I was half as tall as I am now, I often think of that climb when I wonder how any of us got out of childhood alive. But if there is any place you want your ghost to be stuck, The Sea Ranch would be a good one.

During our summers at The Sea Ranch we would hike along the roads in the meadows with names like Cypress Reach or Shepherd's Close and in the hills we would follow Fly Cloud Drive to Timber Ridge to Moonraker Road. We would swim in the Gualala River on the other side of the ridge where the ocean chill was replaced by hotter valley air and go huckleberry picking on old logging roads.

Years later when my grandmother died, John and I went on a backpacking trip around Mount Rainier. For some reason that didn't make sense to either of us, the memorial service wasn't going to be for a couple of months and we both agreed that we needed to grieve *now*, not on a reasonable schedule. Because our grandmother had given us the great outdoors in the form of The Sea Ranch, going to the woods and trails was our memorial to her.

We talked about a lot of things on that three-day trek around the peak of Rainier, but we both agreed that The Sea Ranch was what probably kept us both sane in a crazy childhood. Our parents had gotten divorced and our mother, right or wrong, ended up with all four kids.

We moved around a lot, Cathy went to boarding school, Ben got sucked into the drug scene of the seventies when he was way too young to handle it, John moved back to our dad's and I ended up in and out of foster and group homes.

But The Sea Ranch was always there, even if we weren't together as a family. It was the constant in a world that was never stable and always changing. We would get together in the summers, away from the harshness of the world over the hills, make huckleberry duff, build dams out of sand on the beach, go swimming, and just be kids for a week or two.

So maybe if you visit The Sea Ranch it won't have that same magical, emotional pull that it has for me. Maybe, sometimes, there really is a door in the back of the wardrobe, and it leads to a place that only you can really know, and for me, The Sea Ranch was that place.

Beaches, Softball and Oil Rigs

I ALWAYS REMIND PEOPLE I AM FROM NORTHERN CALIFORNIA, not just California. Northern and Southern California would probably be separate states, except Southern California needs the water from the north, and Northern California needs the money from the south. We'll see what happens as they both run out of those things.

One of my earliest memories is from a family trip to Los Angeles to visit my father's brother's family. My uncle made toy guns from a block of wood and a dowel, which really looked exactly like a block of wood with a dowel in it; but we didn't care. Toys made on demand are always magical.

This is where the emotional scars came from the peanut butter and banana sandwich incident. While the adults ate roast beef inside the house, the kids were ushered onto the back stoop with the sticky sweet sandwich concoction. Bananas? On a sandwich? To my three-year-old tastes, it was just wrong, and seemed somehow like a punishment.

Decades later my mother told me she had no idea we were bothered by it. Our cousins loved peanut butter and banana sandwiches; my aunt probably felt she was giving us a treat. To this day, "peanut butter and banana sandwiches" is the image I evoke to describe something that's just... not quite right.

Southern California is like that, too: not quite right. It has beaches, but unlike The Sea Ranch, the water is warm. It has the largest city in the state, but L.A. is nothing like San Francisco. It's called "California" but it's not the California I grew up in.

It's easy to see where the writers at Star Trek got the idea for the Borg Cube when you fly into LAX -- straight, parallel lines running far into the distance, no sign of anything that hasn't been consumed by the collective below. When Matt Groening moved from Portland to Los Angeles he only thought it appropriate to name his comic strip *Life In Hell* in honor of the city.

There is no way to visit L.A. and not rent a car. Things are just too spread out. I have sat in traffic on I-405, tried to avoid it and ended up sitting in traffic on Sepulveda, headed to the beach to get away from it all and sat in traffic on the Santa Monica Freeway... Sitting in traffic is just something you do in L.A.

I did manage to avoid renting a car when visiting DirecTV. Their offices are right on the edge of LAX, a shorter cab trip than taking the shuttle to the car rental. Standing outside their office and by looking under the elevated highway I could just see the old, stucco building that was the terminal in the days when Bogie and Bacall flew in and out of L.A.

The stars of yesteryear couldn't know that someday Howard Hughes would create Hughes Space and Communications Group right next door, and that it would become DirecTV. Maybe he talked about satellites beaming images to Earth, but they would have thought his idea was either science fiction or the babbling of one of his psychotic breaks that weren't quite as secret as he would have liked.

Of course, there wasn't much around the Hyatt Place in the middle of a block of offices, but when I checked in and checked Google I found the beach was only three miles away. So I did something no one does in L.A.

I walked.

The area around the hotel was what you would expect with business offices and wide busy streets. There was a huge soccer complex with games going on, which surprised me a little, and I passed the home of the LA Lakers, with their sprawling complex of sports buildings and offices.

But as I walked west toward the ocean the big lots with big buildings gave way to subdivisions. Little houses with lawns and yards on residential streets. The roar of the freeway and airport were muted by trees, or perhaps by my surprise that an oasis of livability existed surrounded by so much commercial space.

There were softball games in the city park, and the only word to describe downtown El Segundo is "quaint", with the old shops and restaurants in an almost Norman Rockwell setting. But to the north is the Los Angeles International Airport, to the east, freeways and office complexes.

The southern and western borders of El Segundo take an even worse turn with gigantic tanks of oil, processing plants and old oil rigs still pumping ancient sludge of long dead dinosaurs and rotten plants from the depths of the earth. I crested the hill where the road snaked between two oil refineries and then the ocean was spread below me, just beyond the roaring traffic on the busy street that bordered the sand that led to the water covered with oil tankers parked like SUV's at a Wal-Mart.

This is not the Pacific Ocean I grew up with; it's a crazy Bizarro World Pacific Ocean where the air is filled with the smell of burning petroleum gases and you keep your shoes on or risk stepping on a needle or broken glass. I walked to the edge of the water and looked back at the oil tankers and listened to the roar of the airport in the distance.

With a disappointed sigh and one last glance at the alien ocean, I headed back to my nondescript hotel room by the airport.

Death Valley

THE FABRIC OF THE INNER TENT WAS MOVING IN SYMPATHY with the cold wind whipping around the outer tent in the middle of the night. My traveling companion had brought her two-person tent and I had brought my big, eight-man Coleman tent. We set hers up inside mine with our sleeping bags zipped together to create a king-size canopied bed.

Slipping out of the cocoon of sleeping bags and a warm body, I stood up in the outer tent. The chill of the air moved around as if the walls of the tent were bellows expanding and contracting with the wind.

I poked my head out of the tent and felt my ears and nose immediately burn with the freezing wind. It felt like it was somewhere around zero degrees Fahrenheit, with a wind chill of a million. The stars flickered and winked overhead in the chaotic but clear air.

There was the Milky Way, the backbone of the night, stretching overhead like a cloudy bit of sky, but in the absolute dark and cold of desert there was no question that this was farther away than any cloud on Earth.

My eyes began to blur and hurt in the dry, cold wind. I pulled my head back in, zipping the door closed, and crawled back into the warm bed with the warm woman in the middle of Death Valley.

Christmas break is probably not the best time to go to Death Valley, but the middle of summer would be a dangerous mistake. In late December the nights may kill you with the extreme cold, but the days are in the 50s and 60s -- again, Fahrenheit. In the summer it gets into the 50s, too, but only if you count in Celsius.

The expanse of the valley doesn't feel as desolate or as dead as some places I've been. The ice fields in Norway or the Salt Plains in Utah are far more lifeless than much of Death Valley, with its sage brush and, at least in the winter, grasses and wildflowers.

Distances are difficult to figure in the clear, dry air. We parked at a turnout and while my companion stayed with the car, I decided to hike towards the nearby hills. After about half an hour I began to feel like I was in a Flintstones cartoon; I passed what looked like the same rocks and same bushes over and over and over, never getting any closer to the hills.

I turned back towards the parking area and couldn't make it out in the distance. Another half hour of rocks and bushes and I found the trailhead and our car. I've heard that people get hopelessly lost and run out of food and water because they eyeballed a distance in the desert and packed for a day hike when they were actually heading out for mountains 50 miles away.

On our way back to the cool, wet Northwest we went a little farther south to see the Joshua trees. Heinlein wrote a short story where a group of people fell through a wormhole into what they thought was an alien world, only to discover they were in the Joshua Tree National Park. It's not hard to see how he came up with the idea looking at these weird trunks that look like something Salvador Dali would have painted.

The desert is indeed an amazing place, but I assume so is the surface of Mars. Leaving the extreme temperatures, the tricky distances and the weird plants was almost a relief. Seeing the fog clinging to the redwoods as we neared home reminded me why I chose the ocean and not the desert as my home.

Nowhere Lands

The Sky Club at JFK feels like the lobby of an upscale hotel. There is a huge buffet area, the full bar, and the large, open floor plan with the modern furniture that gleams with leather and chrome. I had put together a plate of food and settled into a chair with a drink when Markie tapped me on my shoulder.

"Come on."

I'm the world traveler, and she was just along using my accumulated reward miles. Obviously she didn't know that I had scoped out the best spot to hang out for our three-hour layover. But I gathered up my stuff and followed her down the hall, around a corner and, impossibly, outside.

Once you're in the airport system you never get to feel the sun or breathe fresh air. There simply aren't outdoor spaces, often there aren't even windows. But leave it to Markie to find the Sky Deck with the colorful tarpaulin awnings, teak furniture and an outside bar looking more like Miami Beach than JFK.

Peering through the shrubs behind our lounging chairs was like peeling away the fantasy. Over the edge I saw a plane with a jetway attached -- we were directly above weary travelers boarding a flight as we sipped our drinks in the sunshine in our hidden oasis.

Sometimes the journey is a chore, and sometimes you get lucky.

The Glamour of Travel

THE PORTLAND TO AMSTERDAM FLIGHT TAKES ABOUT TEN hours, but that's really just a small part of my day. It leaves at about one in the afternoon so I have to get to the Portland airport a little after eleven in the morning, which means I have to leave the house around 10:30 in the morning.

This means I basically have time to get up, shower, get dressed, have some coffee and start the first of my many somewhat anxious periods of waiting while I wait for the cab and worry about whether I remembered to pack everything that I'm going to need for a week in a country with an unfavorable exchange rate and 20% sales tax.

Entering the airport is like immediately leaving Portland. I'm on the borders of another country as I print my ticket from the kiosk -- and I don't mean whatever European destination is showing on my boarding pass. I'm entering the United Federation of Airports.

It doesn't matter that I'll pass through Amsterdam on my way to London, I won't really be in Amsterdam, I'll still be in an airport. They will speak English throughout the trip, although it changes regionally, just as the English they speak in Louisiana is different from the English they speak in New Jersey. There is a common culture with similar food being served in similar ways throughout the Federation. The posted currency might change, but I use the same credit cards and my bank deducts dollars from my account no matter where I am in the system.

I wait in line to pass through security, showing my passport for the first of countless times over the course of my trip. They check my passport and examine my boarding pass like border officers checking a visitor's visa -- having a passport alone isn't enough to gain you access to the UFA.

After collecting my things I realize my anxiety about getting to the airport and getting through the security lines was unnecessary so I get in line for coffee. I don't really know why I do this as it's just another moment for me to worry about how slowly the line is moving, with customers asking questions about the drinks as if they have never ordered coffee before.

Then someone orders something like a double skinny extra pump frapolicious, which brings the line to a halt while the entire staff has to crush ice, go to storage to get the special chilled coffee, grow bananas from seed, and all the other things that go into the construction of a drink that probably has more cumulative worker hours than Boston's Big Dig. They should make those kinds of drinks illegal in airports -- not all of us get to the airport four hours before boarding.

I rush down the concourse, somehow having forgotten that my international flight is, of course, a big plane and therefore at the far end of the terminal. Hot coffee starts to seem like a bad idea as my heart rate and core temperature climb. Then I get to the gate to find that the doors are still closed and people who are waiting to board are sitting in the uncomfortable seats, on the planter boxes, on the floor, leaning on the walls, or wandering aimlessly.

This is another standard point of mild anxiety in my day -- I've made it this far, but there's always the chance the plane won't be able to fly or that it will be delayed interminably and that I, too, will be forced to find a patch of planter box, floor or wall.

Of course I've never actually been delayed on this flight, and we eventually begin to board. I travel light on international trips, not wanting to trust my bags to the underclass of the UFA, so I'm always one of those guys who pushes in early to try to get on board; I want to make sure there is room for my bags (suitcase and messenger bag) in the overhead compartment, preferably an overhead compartment that's actually over my head, not a down-the-aisle-in-the-back-of-the-plane compartment.

Stand in line to show my ticket and passport. Stand in line on the jetway. Say "Hello" to the flight attendant in the doorway. Stand in line in the aisle. "Hello" to the flight attendant standing in a row of seats. Suitcase up. Laptop, Kindle, magazine... Oh, crap, sorry, need to get back into my messenger bag for my headphones. Sit down and wait for a couple hundred more people to do the same.

While I wait for everyone to get settled I send my final text messages and Facebook postings. Maybe by the time you read this WiFi over the Atlantic will be common, but in 2014 it was practically nonexistent, which means I have to prepare myself for ten hours in flight with no Internet, cut off, sequestered, deaf, dumb and blind... at least from a *Matrix* point of view.

Finally we're about ready to push back ("Yes I am willing and able to assist in the event of an emergency..."). The humorous Delta safety video starts to play, with its inside references and a cameo by the flight attendant who was so memorable with her wagging finger a few years ago. Soon there is the somewhat forced socializing with the flight attendant who sits in the jump seat in the exit row, with somewhat forced eye contact and somewhat forced smiles.

And finally, the series of somewhat anxious events that have led me here are over. Now I begin my ten hour flight.

Ten hours strapped in a chair. If you ever ask me what book I would take to a desert island the answer is easy -- a Kindle. Or maybe a nook. I actually carried both on a few trips -- Markie had a nook account and I had a Kindle, so I bought a cheap nook so I could read her books on flights, too.

One problem is getting completely pulled into a book. Or rather, not being pulled into it. I need complete distraction from the family in the middle row who are discovering the bassinette for the first time and can't stop talking about it. I need distraction from that particular slow climb and drop in pitch of the engines. And most of all, I need to ignore the people waiting in line for the toilets -- the extra leg room in the exit row is required for my 34" inseam, but the downside is the wall in front of me has a toilet on the other side.

The drink cart comes by, and I get wine or maybe a gin and tonic. I've never understood people who need to get completely shitfaced on public transportation, but I also know that a mild sedative isn't a bad idea in this environment.

A bit later the first meal comes, which is honestly not that bad. I'm not saying it's good, but I try to pace myself, keeping a bit of bread for the end, setting aside the cookie or brownie to have with a cup of tea when they come through again.

I check the time and I'm less than two hours into the flight. More than a full working day of hours to go. On this leg -- I still have to catch the CityHopper from Amsterdam back to London when this is done. Not that it's going to be done any time soon.

I believe that my distance bicycling days prepared me for international flights. There is no denying that it is an endurance sport. Like when I was trying in vain to ignore my bike computer when I was grinding up the side of a mountain, I have to ignore the clock on my phone or my laptop while I slowly crawl across Canada at five hundred miles an hour.

Eventually I turn to the movies. When I was drinking with colleagues one night in San Jose I mentioned something about *The Lego Movie*.

"Why on earth did you watch *The Lego Movie?*" asked the grey-bearded tech guru.

"I was on a plane."

"Alright then..."

As a fellow world traveler it was the only explanation he needed; you watch amazingly stupid stuff on a plane. I tried watching *Hyde Park on Hudson* or other artsy films, but my brain can't process particularly complex subjects when I'm trying to escape a tiny, crowded universe that offers no physical escape.

You can't really walk the aisles without bumping every third shoulder. You can only go to the toilet so many times, and at some point after three toilets have been shared by that many people for that long you don't really want to go in there unless you absolutely have to.

I write the alphabet with my feet to keep the circulation moving, and on one or two of those trips to the toilet I do old bicycling stretches in the little pass-through that connects the two aisles, but for the most part I just try to keep myself in a mild, self-induced coma.

In the summer months the sun shines for too much of the overnight trip to be allowed into the cabin. The flight crew comes along and closes the window shades, and the universe becomes a little smaller. I find the jazz station on the inflight entertainment and read some more, and then watch another movie.

And there's still five hours to go.

I don't sleep on planes. I might doze a little, but even though this is an overnight flight, my local clock tells me it's just late afternoon. I try to force myself to sleep, but "force" and "sleep" aren't words that go together.

Besides, the little pillow in its disposable polyester sleeve doesn't stay in place when I try to wedge it between my head and the bulkhead. I've tried the Dracula pose so many business travelers seem to have mastered, crossing my arms and leaning back in a lifeless sleep, but then my head snaps up with that ugly little snort that tells me I was starting to snore.

They come through with the ice cream. It's too sweet and the stupid wooden spoon isn't any less stupid because we're flying over the North Atlantic. But I almost always accept the snacks because even though it's true you shouldn't eat out of boredom, there is some boredom where eating isn't just a distraction, it's a mental life preserver.

I try not to laugh out loud at whatever stupid movie I'm watching. Even worse is when I feel myself tearing up at some sentimental scene -- I feel like an invalid with my airplane blanket and my empty ice cream cup while tears well up like a rheumy old man.

But the fatigue of sitting still that long starts to wear on me six or seven hours into the flight.

Breakfast comes through about an hour and a half out from the airport. It's a nasty croissant with ham and cheese; on the flight back it's a nasty ham and cheese sandwich. The oil and the salt and the gummy bread gives me something to do for another fifteen or twenty minutes, although I know I'll regret it later when my stomach wakes up and figures out what I've put in there.

Then it's "daytime" again -- the flight crew asks everyone to open the blinds and bright daylight fills the cabin. Of course we're over the North Sea so there's nothing to see but clouds and water, but the change is striking and there's a new rush to stand in line for the toilets.

We sail in over the coast and the canals with the giant windmills, power-generating windmills like Eastern Oregon, not cute wooden Dutch things. In fact, the landscape is very industrial, but it's land. And then we touch down on that land. And taxi for twenty minutes. I swear the runway is in Rotterdam and we have to drive to Amsterdam...

Seat belts off. Grab my bag. Laptop, Kindle, headphones... do I want to just leave that magazine behind? Wait in line to get off the plane. And out into the bustle of Schiphol.

The longer I have traveled through the complex airline system, the less complex it seems. Like a naturalized citizen, I have started to feel at home when I step into the airport, whether arriving by plane or leaving the foreign strangeness of the place I was visiting, when I step into the terminals of the United Federation of Airports I step into a place whose customs and surroundings are comforting in their familiarity.

I find coffee next to the champagne bar, and while my internal clock says it's eleven at night, it's eight in the morning here. But time doesn't matter -- I'm still in an airport, therefore I'm outside the normal sense of space and time.

I may not have a TARDIS, but traveling by jet plane in the 21st century breaks down any normal concepts of time when I find myself living in the future with the time change from Portland to Europe.

My home is suddenly in another dimension, nine hours in the past and unreachable in any reasonable amount of time without advanced technology. My time machine isn't alien technology powered by a star that has collapsed into a singularity. My time machine is a 767 powered by a jet engine. But if something happens and jets can't fly or I can't get into an airport, time machines and jet planes are equally impossible for me to build.

The Doctor always jiggers his companion's mobile phone so she can call home, no matter the fact that home may be millions of light years and millions of actual years distant. Those conversations with Mum are always a little strained because it's hard to bring context to chit-chat when your frame of reference is so separated.

I'm sure that The Doctor travels with a companion just so he can have someone to talk to who has context in his incredible circumstance. I can post photos and snippets about my trip to Facebook, but most of my friends are living in last night. The instant connection of a "Like" or a comment on my photo is impossible when living in the future.

Of course, photos and notes will never convey the reality of where I am or what I'm seeing. I take photos, I try to write about what I'm seeing, but the chaos and the smells and the energy of being surrounded by people who look different, talk differently and think differently than me is something a Facebook posting will never convey.

Sometimes I succeed in explaining it, but my friends' responses to my interpretation is never the same thing as seeing it together. And whatever my friends and family have to say about my adventures will be tempered by that gap in time and space and will never be the same as turning to a companion at the time and saying, "Did you see THAT?!?"

It turns out that home isn't just where the heart is. It's where your clock is set and where not just your family and closest friends, but where your acquaintances are. The casual interactions with people sharing your time and space make life that much more real.

If I spend too much time in the world of airports and fractured time, it makes the casual connections at home more difficult, while the casual connections with fellow travellers become more real and easier to create.

And so as I sit in Amsterdam I get online after being cut off from home for so long without WiFi and I write and email and text photos from the time and place where I am, hanging onto those connections at home and hoping that I don't become too alien to return to common time and space.

It often feels like I have traveled to another planet, and after sitting for so long in an artificial environment breathing dry, canned air, in a pressurized metal tube to protect me from the unlivable habitat outside the tiny windows, I realize how close we are to actual, commercial space travel.

I shudder to think what we really have to look forward to if air travel is any indication of what space travel is going to be like. I don't think it's going to be like Heywood Floyd's trip to the moon in *2001: A Space Odyssey*. Business Class has bigger seats and more legroom than the livestock section we call Coach, but even that doesn't have as nice of seats or as friendly of hostesses as the Pan Am space clipper.

I feel it's a bad sign for space tourism that one of the most realistic parts of that movie was that Pan Am was the space liner Dr. Floyd took; Pan Am being one of the first traditional airlines to die in the cost-crunching years when air travel turned from luxury accommodations to buses in the sky.

If Delta is an indicator, I think space clippers are going to be less luxurious than cramming twenty people into a 1969 Volkswagen microbus and welding the doors and windows shut. If you're one of those folks who takes Airborne and doesn't turn on the overhead air on a flight for fear of catching a cold... space tourism may not be for you.

Not only that, the whole point of space tourism is to go into orbit and come back down again. It would be like paying a quarter of a million dollars to take an international flight only to find yourself back at the airport where you started. At least after my ten hour ordeal from Portland I was in Amsterdam. Taking off from Dallas and landing again at Dallas is something I have nightmares about. Really.

Even if they build a space station, it's not exactly going to be a luxury destination -- you can probably get the same experience by visiting the Heathrow Yotel. I can get plenty of windowless, cramped, overpriced lodging with no hot water and only airport food right here on Earth.

So, it's not "space travel" that makes me nervous about space tourism, but rather "Space Hospitality." I've seen what we do with expensive travel and limited resources and as long as my expectations are set by airlines and "luxury efficiency hotels," I think I'll keep my head below 40,000 feet.

Anglophile's Paradise

It was 2 a.m. in Tooting Broadway. The tube was closed for the night, so Charlie called a mini-cab for me. It was the driver's first night and he didn't seem to know where Paddington Station was. How you can even be in London and not know Paddington Station was beyond me.

I tried to give him directions through the alcohol, jet lag and my complete lack of knowledge of the city. After the third time around the same roundabout I told him to stop, opened my door, handed him a £20 note and got out.

London is surprisingly empty at 2:30 in the morning. I walked the dark streets listening to the night birds whistle in the shadows of the trees overhead. Every now and then I would check the map on my phone and find that the curving streets of London had pushed me away from my target and I would have to try to find a new way around the buildings and gated parks.

Soon I saw the familiar shape of a proper cab. As he took me to my hotel he ranted about how Boris was ruining taxis in London by letting anyone with a satnav and a car pretend to be a driver.

"Always best to use a real cab, sir."

London

I HAD FLOWN INTO LONDON ENOUGH TIMES THAT I HAD developed a routine. It doesn't matter whether I take the flight from Portland to Amsterdam and then a jaunt back to London, or go from Portland to Minneapolis to London, I always get in around ten in the morning.

My internal clock still reads 2 a.m., and despite snoozing on the ten hour flight, it begins to feel like pulling an all-nighter at this point.

Grab my roll-aboard and wait for the people in front of me on the plane to move. Deboard, then walk quickly past the people who are trying to figure out where to go -- it doesn't pay to get behind them in immigration.

The first time I went to London I only had a few stamps in my passport. There were a lot of questions about the purpose of my visit, where I was staying, what is it I really do for a living, who would I see while in London...

By the end of the year with my passport full of stamps the conversation went along the lines of, "Are you here for business, sir?"

"Always."

"And what do you do?"

"I run a technology platform for managing complex API infrastr..."

"That's fine, sir." {STAMP}-{STAMP} "Enjoy your stay."

Then it's a few more winding hallways and into the baggage claim area. The only time I checked a bag to London was when I was bringing in a bottle of rye whiskey for a friend. I swear my bag was the last one off the carousel that day because of what I imagine was a discussion between a baggage handler and a supervisor that ended with, "Put it back."

I quickly bypass the confused-looking people guarding what bags they have retrieved while their companions search for their missing luggage. Another reason to avoid checked baggage when traveling alone -- no one to watch my stuff while looking for my other stuff. Another hallway marked "Nothing to Declare," then, exit through the gift shop and I'm out into the UK proper.

Well, I'm still in Heathrow. But I could walk outside and hail a cab if I wanted to spend far too much money and waste an inordinate amount of time in traffic. I head for the trains.

Quite often there is a person in a purple uniform just inside the Duty Free shop who will sell you a ticket on the Heathrow Express. If you're lucky enough to grab one of them you can have a flimsy receipt and be on your way to the lifts, otherwise you're stuck in a queue of people trying to figure out why the machine won't take their credit cards, and how much, exactly, is £21 in U.S. dollars?

The Heathrow Express doesn't usually go to Terminal 4, so the first train I board goes about two minutes and I have to get off again. Then there's about a ten minute wait, and... finally... it's off to Paddington.

The upbeat music plays in the modern rail cars with white and purple lighting making it feel almost like an upscale restaurant, except for the complete lack of food service. It's almost eerily chipper and I wouldn't be surprised to find Cybermen stepping out of the vestibules ready to upgrade the passengers.

The train speeds along a track that feels like it's been there for over a hundred years, and most definitely has. Dull brownish red brick houses flick by, occasional structures that might be left over from mining or deep space radar, and just before I'm ready to fall asleep the chipper music is back with the clear British announcer telling us we have reached the end of the line and please collect your belongings and mind the gap and thank you ever so much for riding with us.

When I first saw Paddington Station I was a bit disappointed. I don't know what I expected from the station where they found Paddington Bear, but the enormous hangar-like space with the shops and a Burger King at the end wasn't it. I think Brits romanticize mundane places, and Americans then put our own romantic notions on top of that.

Rolling my suitcase behind me, I leave the station and really enter London for the first time on my trip. The double decker busses and black London cabs are everywhere. The street crossings have warnings painted on the pavement to "Look Right!" or just as often, "Look Left!" Just because they drive on the left side of the road doesn't mean the streets always behave that way.

It's easy to get turned around in London. The streets curve, turn into alleyways or end altogether in a T intersection. But as with anything, once I figured it out, I can walk like a Londoner and I'm quickly at my hotel.

Of course, it's only about noon and the hotel isn't ready for me. So I check my luggage with the concierge and head to Hyde Park.

Sunday afternoons in the spring and summer find the park filled with people walking, running, cycling, playing catch or just sitting on the lawns enjoying the day. The mix of languages was startling the first time I walked through Hyde Park. Russian families seem to take a walk in the park on Sunday as some sort of civic or familial duty. Middle Eastern languages abound, and of course all of Europe is represented.

There just don't seem to be many people speaking English.

Finding a cafe by the waters of the Serpentine I try to stay away from the alcoholic beverages. My entire goal is to stay awake until a reasonable time to go to bed so as to get on local time as quickly as possible. But the Pimm's often calls to me on a summer day and then I just have to have a bit of cake to help absorb the alcohol.

I have tried having the Natural History Museum as part of my first-day routine, but the crowds and noise are just a bit much on my frayed system after being awake for over 24 hours and I usually wander back to the hotel to settle in.

Around four in the afternoon I lose consciousness. I try not to, but I'll be sitting in a comfortable chair with my laptop and suddenly wake up around five or five thirty. I'll curse and try to shake the cobwebs and go find something for dinner.

I can usually find a roast in a pub on Sundays, and I love a good roast with a bit of pudding, but at some point I started going to the inexpensive take-away Asian places like Wagamama. A container of something with noodles in it and a beverage, and I head back to my room to watch a bit of BBC... okay, Channel 4... okay, really YouTube...

If I make it to 8:00 I feel pretty good about being on my way to local time. The problem is that my body now thinks it's noon, and I find myself poking around Facebook until 10 or 11, when I tell myself, "I really gotta get some sleep if I'm working tomorrow..." and then I'm out.

In the morning I iron a shirt, grab my gear and head to the office. I'll hit a Costa along the way for a cappuccino or latte, and stroll through Paddington to the new, steel and glass offices in One Kingdom Street just north of the station.

The day is like many days with clients, although the breaks have tea and biscuits, as well as almost palatable coffee. I have to remember to pronounce "router" like "rooter" which, for some reason, seems less dirty to the British ear. And when the day is done, I chat with my London colleagues in the back office until eventually someone pipes up with, "Pub?" and we're off.

I come from a town that drinks. We drink a lot. I mean, if an alcoholic landed on my block on an average Tuesday they might say to my neighbors and me, "Um… yeah… well, I gotta get up in the morning…" But Londoners have taken the evening pint to a whole different level. What we think of as "enabling" they think of as "just being polite."

It started one night in the office complex in Paddington with four of us. The sales guy got the first round. They actually had something called a "Yakima Red" on tap at Smith's; it was a passable red lager made with hops from the Columbia Valley in Washington and malt from Denmark. 4.6% according to the tap, 4.0% on Beeradvocate.com, but alcohol content doesn't matter as much as volume.

Four of us…. That means we were in for four rounds. It's only polite.

I got the fourth round, which meant I was picking up the tab for my pint that ticked the "half gallon" mark, which honestly, is probably the top of my comfortable drinking. And keep in mind, these are Imperial pints -- 20 ounces to our 16... so it's really a pint more than a half gallon by my standards.

I have to say it's nice to be out with Brits because they drink a lot like Portlanders -- we don't mean to go beyond that comfortable drinking limit, but it would be rude to head out when there is someone who might want another round.

Then the office manager showed up. It would only be polite to have another round to keep him company. It's not his fault he had to work late, after all. "Whatch'a drinking?" he asks, naturally. So he bought round five -- which means the half gallon mark was left far behind without really thinking about it.

It gets a bit hazy after that… The orderly passing of the rounds from person to person fell by the wayside and the drinking turned into a competitive sport the way the tribes of the Northwest, such as the Yakima whose namesake filled my glass, compete with potlatch. "I will bestow upon you this slightly toxic beverage as an honor upon you, but it is only an honor if you drink it. All of it."

I knew I was in trouble when the shots of whiskey started showing up. As the token American it was only polite to have the

Makers Mark, it being cultural and all that. The second shot just sort of showed up, so I wasn't sure who I would offend by not drinking it, but I was sure it would be someone. The fact it was accompanied by another Yakima Red was no one's fault after all, I had been drinking them all night.

Then this woman who wasn't part of our company slipped into the circle. Irish, growing more so the more she drank. Again, it would have been rude to move on at that point, even if I did have to step away from the conversation for a moment to make sure that my peristaltic waves weren't reversing.

Eventually the women refused enough rounds that the party started to break up. Thank God for women -- men would keep pushing each other into another round, but at some point the balance of being polite to the women balances out the politeness of keeping up with the other drinkers.

After all no one really wants to get drunk. Everyone is just being polite.

My whole routine changed when Markie came to London with me. My work routine was suddenly interrupted by a social schedule -- somehow Markie scheduled drinks and outings with friends and acquaintances I didn't know we had, and then she was up to Leicester by train for a day to visit some friends in the country while I lectured in a windowless conference room in Paddington. I think she missed her country and era by a few hundred years and six thousand miles -- she would have made a brilliant Lady of leisure.

Our rather "flamboyant" director friend was in London from Portland to take in as much theatre as possible and insisted on showing us Harrods. Markie and I had taken a cab over from our hotel in Marylebone -- I discovered riding in cabs with a female companion in London is different than riding in cabs with a male, business companion. The stereotypical "darlings" and "luvs" rolled from the cabbie like he had been scripted for Dick van Dyke in *Mary Poppins.*

A quick lunch with Jon at an Asian takeaway, which interrupted the classic London moment with a reality London moment of plastic containers heated in the microwave, and then he whisked us into Harrods.

The first rooms we saw were like Macy's on steroids. A big room filled with perfume counters. Then another room filled with men's suits. Then the shoes... Each room was like a department store for a single department. I went downstairs to the men's salon to inquire about a manicure and even without doing the math on the exchange rate it made my nails retract on their own.

Then it got more intense.

The food rooms put Willy Wonka to shame; yes the chocolate room defies description and we did not get out of there without a purchase, but Wonka didn't have a charcuterie next to a boulangerie that adjoined a room filled with fruits and vegetables.

Back through the perfume room we descended the Egyptian Escalator. I'm fairly certain ancient Egyptians did not have escalators, but they would not have been disappointed with these ornate moving staircases. And, at the bottom of the escalator is a memorial.

There, in a lucite pyramid was a wine glass with lipstick on the rim. It was Diana's last glass of wine before the fateful car crash in Paris. A life-size sculpture of Dodi and Diana dancing hand in hand with the inscription, "Innocent victims" sits between the Egyptian escalators. I wasn't sure whether to be appalled or amused, but the silly giggle that kept slipping out settled the matter.

Dodi Fayed's family bought Harrods in 1985, and of course his father should be able to erect a memorial to his son and his son's girlfriend, although it's quite clear the Queen would prefer something a little less commercial and a bit more understated than relics and idolatry. The fact the Al-Fayed family sold the store in 2010 and that the memorial remains is probably more a testament to foot traffic than respect.

We ascended from the memorial, gliding on the Egyptian escalator and found our way to the Prosecco bar. This is just one of two sparkling bars in the department store -- we decided the Champagne Bar in the International Fashion collection was just a little too much, even for our champagne tastes.

And directly across the aisle from the Prosecco bar was the Ice Cream Bar with the staff in the black and white suits with the long French bistro aprons and with the chandelier made of tulip ice cream glasses, and with combinations of ice cream and syrups and fruit and whipping cream and nuts and little teddy bear cookies... It's never too late to have a happy childhood, especially after a couple of glasses of bubbly.

We browsed the bookstore, took pictures with the seven-foot-tall teddy bears, peeked in at the Middle East Desk with its understated opulence and clearly stated professionalism, until it all became overwhelming and it was time to go.

The uniformed doorman in the long green coat let us out and gave us directions. Jon had to get to the West End and we wanted to do some sightseeing along the Thames, so we took the tube together until it was time to part ways, saying our goodbyes movie style through the closing doors of the train and waving as it sped off into the tunnel.

We came out of the Underground at Westminster, surfacing into a crowd of people next to Big Ben with the crush of cars and buses making the street look more like India than London. The sounds of a bagpiper on Westminster Bridge drifted over the crowds only to get lost in the singing of a football team's fight song that came from the open deck of a tourist bus filled with men in striped scarves.

Across the Thames is The London Eye, the giant bicycle wheel with gondola cars surrounded by the theme-park style London Dungeon, food courts and video arcades. Riding the slow turn of The Eye is worth it, if you can keep from hyperventilating fording the crowds of tourists getting there.

It was Christmastime on the Queen's Walk as we left "theme park London" and strolled east into the stalls of the Christmas Village. I wanted to complain about the commercialization of Christmas in November but it's kind of tough when you're in a country that doesn't have Thanksgiving, and they do it so well it's hard to be angry for long.

The cold wind blew up the river as we continued into the darkness, crossing under bridges and cutting around blocks of flats until we found the Tate Modern. Rooms with empty frames, half-silvered mirrors and other ironic art made me start looking at the directories to find the bar that I knew had to be in there somewhere.

The bar was packed.

We squeezed into a nice spot by the window overlooking the Thames with St Paul's peeking above the buildings of the north bank and shared a bottle of Ninkasi. Not the Ninkasi that Markie's nephew brews in Oregon but a brew by the Wild Beer Company in Westcombe. Sometimes you have to try things just because of the randomness of association. It was a nice, soft saison, and fit the museum bar atmosphere and our drinking schedule perfectly.

Markie had been having trouble with the beers in London -- too warm and flat, but she kept trying them because she liked the flavor. She's a 5'2" American so she probably shouldn't have been surprised when a barkeeper handed her a beer and said, "Careful with that, it's 4.5%"

Londoners don't really understand Northwesterners and their beers. They think all Americans drink Budweiser, or as the boys of Monty Python said, beer that is like "making love in a canoe" -- fucking close to water.

We strolled the Thames, taking a selfie of the two of us with the Tower Bridge in the background. We took the tour of the

Tower Bridge, and were forced to stand in front of a green screen so they could try to sell us a photo of what looked like a selfie of us standing in front of the Tower Bridge.

There were other nights and other pubs and other parts of London; we narrowly escaped trivia night in Hammersmith in a pub on the river, something we probably would have been terrible at with British pop references. We ended up in a pub with low ceilings and a fireplace and a dog curled up by the bar as we chatted with a couple we had met at a party in Portland.

One night we went to a little Polish restaurant in South Kensington that I had discovered with my friend Charlie on an earlier visit. In World War II South Kensington was constantly bombed and the wealthy had moved out, so the Polish refugees moved in. At one time the neighborhood was filled with Polish restaurants, but only this one survived the repatriation of the wealthy South Kensingtonians.

I had always thought Polish food would be something like borscht and boiled potatoes. And, yes, there were beets and potatoes, but they were the most amazing beets and potatoes I've ever had. The delicacy of the sauces, the range of flavors, and everything flowed perfectly.

Then there's the vodka. Lightly infused with honey or lavender or coriander or really any flavor you can think of. As I've said, I don't drink to get drunk, but when you have flavors that dance on your tongue and warm your belly like these chilled shots of nirvana, it's difficult to stay sober.

Fortunately I didn't lose Markie on the train, although there was that moment where the doors nearly closed with her on the wrong side as we were both rather unfocused after losing count of the shots of vodka.

Then it was time to take the Heathrow Express back to the airport where you find that leaving London is almost harder than getting in. Heathrow is the only airport in the world where I have had to take every liquid out of my toiletries bag and put them in a clear zip-lock bag. Yes, you're supposed to do that everywhere, but no one ever really cares so long as they can see things on the X-ray. Unless you're at LHR.

One time I missed a small tube of mosquito repellent that had gone to more airports and countries than I can remember. My bag came out of the X-ray and was shunted off to one side where I couldn't get to it and I had to wait for an interminable amount of time until a guard brought it up and asked me to supervise while she searched my bag. Then, tiny plastic bottle removed, my bag went through again, and I struggled to get to my gate.

But most times there is the weird purgatory in the shopping mall that is Terminal 4 while you wait to find out what gate your plane will depart from. I've never figured out if it's because they can better manage the number of people milling around gates that they keep your gate secret until just before boarding time, or if it's to force you to shop in the Duty Free mall. I admit to having been tempted by a £600 jacket but the most I've ever really spent was £30 on lunch.

I love visiting London. The free museums alone could keep me busy for a year of weekends, and then there's the proper ale, Sunday roasts and, if I don't want to do the English, plenty of excellent international food. But I if I had to live there, I think I would fancy the idea of having a house in the country and heading to London only for business or entertainment.

Megacities aren't really conducive to quiet nights and moonlight, which may be more important to me than all the wonders of London.

Manchester

ONE OF THE GUYS AT THE CONFERENCE ROOM TABLE QUIPPED, "Manchester is the birthplace of the industrial revolution and it has never really recovered." He was a local, born and bred in the North, so he could say it, and was saying it almost by way of apology for his home town.

Where London feels like a melting pot of languages and people, Manchester feels like the England we see on BBC America and PBS and it sounds like it, too. My colleagues in London warned me that I wouldn't be able to understand a word the Northerner's say, but it turned out to be easier that the mish-mash of accents in London.

Of course there was the night I stepped into the lift followed by a local woman decked out for the evening in a sparkly black dress with her hair done up and just enough makeup that she was on the classy side of tartish. She was doused in perfume, something women in the scent-free world of the Pacific Northwest never do, and she had been drinking the way the English do.

Some series of words came from her mouth, and for the life of me I have no idea what she said. She could have been asking me what time it was or if I wanted to go back to her room with her. I'll never know. And then she stepped off the lift with a lyrical, "Well, goodnight then!"

It might not have been her accent that kept me from understanding her; I admit I was a little overwhelmed with the overpowering femininity of her. Women in the U.S. just don't glam it up for a night out... and I wish they would a little...

Manchester is a city of stone and iron with seemingly identical Gothic church towers in every direction. Old, utilitarian buildings that once housed sweatshops now house pubs and restaurants. The Northern Quarter's cobbles and low stone buildings feel like an old war zone during the daytime when the metal shutters are drawn down and the streets are empty.

I was in the north of England for two weeks and as I unpacked I realized I had forgotten socks. I might be able to get away with no socks for a week in India, but, I didn't think khakis and huaraches were going to cut it for meetings in Manchester and Wales.

Next to the old buildings of the Northern Quarter is a mall. Different cities have different kinds of shopping malls, some are broad streets that have been closed to traffic allowing you to stroll and shop and maybe have coffee or tea in open-air cafes. Some are old buildings that have been turned into indoor shops.

And some are just shopping malls like every city in America has. The Manchester Arcade is one of those, although I have to wonder if it was designed or just grew over time. It felt almost like a Mobius strip as I walked along the shops on different levels... I must have gone around the place three times before I found the H&M.

Along the way I stopped into Waterstones and got a British interior design magazine for Markie (later proving that "British interior design" is an oxymoron), listened to some students playing Mozart, and got a latte at Costa. As much as I hate shopping malls, I was surprised at how long I was able to stay entertained while lost in its labyrinth.

By the time I had finished buying socks, I discovered that it was too late to get dinner in a proper restaurant. I went back out into the night and found myself in the old part of the city well into the drinking hour. The previously shuttered Northern Quarter had become a club district with young men yelling at other young men, and young women roaming in packs looking for some yelling young men.

The best-looking spot for some takeaway was a brightly-lit shop selling kebabs. A group of teens sat in a booth to one side looking glazed and subdued and obviously trying to focus after a night of drinking, while their one, coherent friend shuttled food to them from the counter.

My order came up and I took it back to my hotel, cutting through an alley where a guy was relieving himself on the wall while I navigated the splashes of vomit.

This is the other side of the "polite drinking..."

If binge drinking was an Olympic sport the Brits would medal every time (although, to be honest, the Russians would hold the Gold). British drinkers start young, and they drink hard. This drinking isn't pleasant rounds of lager at the pub, it's massive amounts of beer and shots of Goldschlager or equally nasty stuff.

The British government recently suggested that two nights off after a night of binge drinking could really help the liver -- none of the American, "WARNING: Alcohol is dangerous to your health." It's more of a, "Hate to be a bother, but perhaps you should stop vomiting before you start drinking again..." Not that either form of government warning is going to change anyone's drinking habits.

The next day I worked with the clients until late afternoon and then set off to find a proper football stadium. This is Manchester, after all, home of Manchester United, one of Beckham's old teams. It's also home to the Manchester City Football Club, and they play in the city stadium, which was in walking distance.

I felt self-conscious following the girl in the short skirt and high heels, even if I did enjoy the effect. She was about a half a block ahead of me, and she kept turning down the same streets Google Maps told me to take. Maybe the PhDs in Mountain View had created a new routing feature for lecherous men.

Soon I found more young women and girls walking in the same direction, also decked out in their "night on the town" outfits. Then I heard the noise from the stadium -- there wasn't a football match that night but there was an event... A One

Direction concert. As a lone, middle-aged guy with a greying beard, surrounded by girls dressed to get the attention of a boy band... I suddenly felt very awkward.

Then I saw the mums and I didn't care about being awkward. The woman who had derailed me in the lift was nothing compared with these Real Housewives of Manchester. I had always thought you had to go to places like Miami Beach or Las Vegas to see women dressed to the nines for a night out, but here in the parking lot of the City of Manchester stadium were more high heels and tight dresses than on a catwalk in Paris.

When American mothers take their girls to a concert they wear sweatpants or jeans and hang out in the parking lot or go home for a couple of hours. When women in Northern England take their girls to a boy band concert, they gather their friends, dress up, drink some champagne and make a night of it.

I think it turned out to be a much better day to visit the stadium than if a football match was on with beer-soaked hooligans.

I spent my final day in Manchester walking around aimlessly, which is how I often find the really cool random stuff in a town. But not Manchester. For a city that's been around since the Romans it has a lot of ugly, 1970s office blocks. In fact, most of the architecture comes from much later than the Industrial Revolution, making it feel more like Philadelphia or Boston; old by U.S. standards, but hardly a Roman village.

The mix of decaying buildings that were supposed to be modern when they were built forty years ago sitting alongside stained stonework from the 1700s reflects Manchester trying to recover from its industrial past. Sometimes it tries to erase the blight and other times tries to preserve the history. The result is a jarring hodgepodge of the worst of both worlds.

I don't know why Chinatown surprised me. The idea of Chinatown must be more a Chinese invention than an American one, but somehow I never thought there would be Chinatowns outside America, let alone in the North of England. It was somehow more familiar to me than the shopping centers and nightclubs and reminded me of the Chinatown I grew up with in San Francisco.

I got a steamed bun from a dour Chinese man at an outdoor counter and kept walking.

The neo-Gothic spires of the Manchester Town Hall looked like a scaled-down version of Parliament in London. Here, I thought, was history that must run deep. Only Google told me it was built in 1894, a last hurrah of the Victorian era.

I regret not taking tea in one of the shops with the full tea trays of cakes and other sweets, but while I'm willing to ask a prostitute for lunch recommendations in Amsterdam, I found myself a little worried about decorum in a place that presented things that well in a shop that may have been there since the 1600s.

I found myself thinking, "Is a lone man even allowed in? Or is it just tea for the ladies in the big city from the village?" Which is to say, I probably grossly overthought it.

Saturday morning came and I had the weekend to kill before meeting with my next client just outside of Chester. I had a proper English breakfast complete with grilled tomatoes and blood pudding that looked like the kind of brown bread you get from a can but tasted like salty sausage. Then I dragged my suitcase over to the old rail station that was impossible to see with all the construction as they erased a bit of the old Manchester and replaced it with something bright and modern that is sure to fade.

They weren't getting rid of the giant map of the Lancashire and Yorkshire Railway system made of brick and enamel that paid homage to the centuries of rail service that connects England to this day. The trains are electric, with small commuter carriages, not the cabins like you see in *Harry Potter's* Hogwarts Express. But for £4.50 the price couldn't be beat.

The train ran along an elevated track out of Manchester, and soon I was in the English countryside, looking at a wall of dirt as the train ran along in its dry canal, keeping the noise of its passage from the quiet villages it serviced. More people got on than off, and soon it was hard to stand, and hard to breathe from the heat and closeness of so many people.

Peering over the heads of the packed car, I got a glimpse of a brick yard with wires overhead coming from all directions as different lines converged. Then the walls came closer together and we stopped on a platform where the crush of people pressed out of the doors leaving me alone in the car to retrieve my bag from the rack.

I had arrived in Liverpool.

Liverpool

Seagulls flew overhead while a band played on the lawn where carts and stalls were selling food and beer. The passengers from the cruise ship crowded the Princess Dock waving at family already, or still, on board the giant ship sitting in the waters where the River Mersey meets the Irish Sea.

If you're picturing Edwardian garb and a brass band, you need to change costumes and music. This is 2014 with T-shirts and electric guitars.

I walked along the dock in late May feeling the sea breeze and enjoying the sun and I wondered how I could have forgotten that Liverpool was a seaside town. The White Star line was based in Liverpool, and even if the Titanic never visited the port, the Lusitania did. This was the heart of shipbuilding, the gateway to the world. In fact, this is where the U.S. Embassy was until the end of World War II.

Unlike Manchester, Liverpool recovered from the Industrial Revolution. Or, rather, it retired. After the war they politely asked the U.S. to move the embassy to London and quietly turned from shipbuilding to management and financial services and tourism.

The old shipbuilding docks are reflecting pools for restaurants and shops and the big Museum of Liverpool which houses the expected collection of bits of clay pots, Roman tools, and steam engines as well as an unexpected exhibit about April Ashley – one of the first people in the world to undergo gender reassignment surgery.

Of course, the shop signs and museums won't let you forget this is the birthplace of The Beatles. The sign for "Elvis and Us" with the Fab Four and Elvis on a stylized sign still confuses me, but then, most tourist attractions confuse me.

The Cavern Quarter is touristy in a different way; by day the shops sell shirts, hats, fuzzy slippers and other knickknacks emblazoned with every variation of the Beatles. The life-size bronze sculpture of the lads lounging over a doorway makes the shop entrance look almost like a mausoleum, and the huge pictures of young Beatles make me think of the Baby Jesus at Christmastime, adding to the shrine-like quality of the street.

But by night, the quarter feels like the red light district in Amsterdam. Drunk gangs of young men and women roam the streets, often clad in identical T-shirts with phrases like "Stu's Stag" or "Lisa's Hen Party" as they try to create their personal version of *The Hangover*. Music blares from every window and doorway while prostitutes give me questioning looks as they try to decide if I would be interested in their services.

I wasn't interested in bursting an eardrum in a club, or breaking my wallet visiting the new Cavern Club where a Beatles look-alike band pretends it's 1962 on the original stage in a not-exactly original space. It seemed almost like a theme park ride, although I admit I had that "it's so bizarre maybe I should" moment... almost.

Instead, I went to find a proper pub.

When I was in Manchester one of the guys told me if there was one thing to see in Liverpool it was the bathrooms at The Philharmonic Dining Rooms, and the beer selection wasn't supposed to be that bad either. It was a mile or so from the Cavern Quarter, so I started walking.

Out of the twisting cobbles of Mathew Street, into the broad, modern open-air shopping district where shops like Forever 21 and L'Occitane compete for your attention along with McDonald's and Marks + Spencer... I eventually escaped into "real Liverpool" or at least the Liverpool not dominated by international brands.

I passed a pub near the train station where people were sitting on the curb with their pints -- not on chairs mind you but actually with their feet in the gutter, but it wasn't the pub I was heading for. I passed a casino with its flashing lights and promises for big winnings. I passed a bar where I swear they were singing country-western karaoke, which should be enough of a deterrent for anyone. And I kept walking.

Then I came across the church with no roof. It had been hollowed out by a firebomb in 1941 and was never repaired. I always think of the Blitz as a London thing, but Liverpool was attacked regularly, too, being the main manufacturer of British war machines it was an obvious target and maybe one of the reasons they didn't really want to be part of the world stage after the war.

The bombed-out church has become a kind of community arts center, with a stage under the open sky where priests once gave benediction and a lawn surrounded by flowers where the parishioners once knelt in their pews and received the blessings of the priest. In a small vestibule, still bearing its stone roof off the north transept there was an art installation with carvings of cars in tiles entitled *Temple to the Sacred Automobile*. In the south transept were port-a-potties.

Not really a House of God any longer, but it was a heck of a Vacation Home of God. They host bands and sometimes, like that day, a priest will come and hold a service under the sky and amongst the flowers inside the Gothic walls and arched windows open to the city.

But the bombed-out church wasn't the most interesting church in the neighborhood. As I climbed the street towards the pub I looked to the north and saw an alien spacecraft which turned out to be a Catholic church -- a cone the size of a city block topped with a glass cylinder that, in turn, was topped by a wire mesh. I might have guessed "telecommunications company from the 50s," but never a Catholic church.

And to the south, with no misconceptions of the nature of the edifice, was the massive Anglican Liverpool Cathedral.

Looking like a slightly over-rendered, ancient structure from *The Lord of the Rings* or some other computer-generated landscape, the Liverpool Cathedral was too real to be real. The haze effect was a little too high and the scale was a little too perfect to be believable for its size, as if a lazy 3D graphics artist had stretched a standard model to fit the script's needs for a gigantic church.

Only it wasn't any more computer-generated than the rest of my life... although how much of my life is computer generated remains to be determined -- this could have just been a glitch in the Matrix. The path to the cemetery below the church was lined with tombstones and when I reached the bottom of the pit and looked up the tower of the Cathedral loomed overhead, impossibly large.

The pit was at least two stories deep, with broken and worn tombstones scattered about the grassy floor. It had been a quarry for hundreds of years before becoming a cemetery in the 1800s. A sheer wall ran along the base of the church on one side and another wall ran below a quiet street on the other.

Tunnels leading away from the church on the far wall were blocked up by old brick and gave the impression that the quarry had been the scene of some horrible religious games where masses of people died while clawing for escape at impassable exits -- which wasn't true at all, but an old graveyard in an ancient quarry has a particular effect on my imagination.

I emerged from the pit through a purple haze wafting from a small group of guys lounging near the gate and I headed down the street past a collection of concrete luggage that had been placed on the sidewalk in what I assume was an art installation. By this time, Liverpool had become so surreal to me that it could have been from a passenger who had thought they had been cursed when their luggage turned to stone and kept them from the maiden voyage of the Titanic.

By this time I was in real need of a pub and came to the Phil.

Sherlock Holmes prefered a "seven-per-cent" solution of cocaine. The Victorian architect who designed the Philharmonic Dining Rooms obviously prefered his solution a little more concentrated. The giant stone building with its rounded windows and turret running up the second and third floors was covered with carvings and balustrades. Copper domes and stone roof spikes adorned the top, and my overall impression was of the kind of dark whimsy a drug addict has when coming down after a particularly long trip into altered states.

But no one really talks about the architecture. They talk about the toilets.

Along one side of the men's room under the small windows are a half dozen five-and-a-half-foot-tall urinals carved from a rust-colored marble with shocks of white that blend into an intricate setting of tilework on the floor and walls. The narrowness of the room means being butt-to-butt with the guy pissing while you wash your hands; but then, I noticed a lot of guys didn't bother with that extra step.

Somewhere in the world there is a photo of me standing at the urinal, probably with that vacant, almost blissful look that men get when relieving themselves. Tourists just can't wait for the toilets to be unoccupied in such a busy pub and just snap the photo for the family album regardless of who is doing what at the time.

I had a couple of pints and enjoyed the dark wood and stained glass in the different rooms of the pub and then walked back to my hotel by the water, past the burnt-out church, past the other pubs and bars, and back through the Cavern Quarter, shaking my head "no" with the bemused but sad smile I find myself wearing when a pretty young woman tries to catch my eye with a similar bemused but sad smile.

Falling asleep while looking out the window into the darkness of the waters of the River Mersey and the sea, I thought about how the Liverpool I expected and the Liverpool I met were such different things.

It would take me a long time to reconcile the two.

The Wall at Chester

AFTER A COUPLE OF WEEKS IN NORTHERN ENGLAND, MY EAR heard distinctly American accents while I was having coffee and cake on a patio built on a 2,000-year-old wall next to a 700-year-old church. The girl was bored with the history, the dad needed to make a call to the office later in the day, and the mother was trying to keep it all together.

It turned out they were Canadians from Toronto, which meant the time change wasn't as hard for them for either sleep or making calls home. But even though we weren't nationally, geographically, or even culturally the same people, we talked the same brand of English and they seemed to be as happy to hear a familiar accent as I was.

I had all day Sunday to kill before heading to Ewloe to sit in a conference room the next day and talk about how to use technology with a coupon company. So I decided to walk the Wall. It was only a two mile loop around the city, and if I didn't stop I could be done in less than an hour.

It took me a little bit longer... well, it took me quite a bit longer. I stopped. A lot.

I left the cafe by the old church and started along the pavers of the old wall and soon I found myself heading down a small stairway in a rocky corridor which opened onto a high street. It was a perfect June day and the street was packed with shoppers and street musicians.

The shops were a mix of local retailers with the occasional Disney store, housed in rows of Tudor buildings that had been built on Roman ruins. My American mind again flashed to places like Disney World and the small town of Leavenworth, Washington, where they create a facade of wooden gables and steeply pitched roofs that hide a rebar and cement structure inside.

But these buildings have housed shops for six hundred years; where you take your computer to be repaired or buy that Stephen King novel there might have once been a cobbler or a weaver. People whose titles honestly included "monger" or "peddler" worked in these shoppes, and they had the olde "e" because it was the newe "e" at the time.

I returned to the wall, climbing up another narrow stairway by a city gate where Roman soldiers had scurried while fighting the British tribes and later where Lord Byron failed to hold the city in the Civil War. On either side of the wall shoppers milled around the stores where men had fought and died over thousands of years.

The Roman Legion was marching in the Amphitheatre when I arrived. Families picnicked around the sandy basin of the arena and tents were set up where women were weaving and armorers fitted soldiers with plate and mail. It may have been one of my temporal disconnects when I become unstuck in time, but the women on the lawn wore jeans and halter tops and the Legate was issuing commands in English.

After a chat with a Roman soldier about the merits of chain mail over plate armor, I continued along the wall with a bucolic view over the flowing waters of the River Dee bordered by green lawns on the far side and a church spire poking above the trees. I half expected to see people in Regency costumes surrounded by cameras and lighting as it was a perfect setting for a BBC period piece.

More wall, then a castle which, after seeing so much antiquity, was just another big building made from huge bricks of rock, and then I found the wall turning into a sidewalk along a street with houses on the city side and a drop off to a large open field on the north. What had once been a harbor when the Romans occupied Chester is now the oldest horse racecourse in the UK with races dating back to the 1600s.

It wasn't hard to imagine the bowl-shaped field filled with water, but it was hard to imagine it being a harbor, until I thought about the ships of the first century; tiny boats even when compared with Mississippi sternwheelers that ply shallow muddy water to this day. The Roman merchant ships could have easily come the ten miles up the River Dee from the sea until the river slowed and started to fill with silt.

The long Sunday walk had made me hungry and thirsty, and just across from the entrance to the racecourse was a wide, open lawn leading up to a pub called The Architect. It felt almost like a miniature country club with groups of people lounging on the lawn in chairs or around low tables.

The pub itself was a Georgian freehouse with just enough stuff on the walls to still be a pub, but much nicer than the pubs I had been to in London or Manchester. There's something about cask ale and a proper Sunday roast I can't resist, nor did I.

Stuffed on beef and potatoes and Yorkshire pudding, and sloshing a bit from the beer, I continued my trek along the Chester wall. The wall that had stood for two millennia took me over the railway tracks which had been cut through the wall a mere 175 years ago, then past Bonewaldestorne's Tower and then back over the tracks. The tower that once protected the walled city is now isolated in its own enclosure protected by Merseyrail.

As I came back to where I started, there was one more view of the ancient Roman wall I knew I had to see. About the time the American Colonies were fighting the King's Army, the people of Chester were breaking the solid, stone bedrock below the city to connect the River Dee to Nantwich some twenty miles away; the result is a deep canyon with the old wall on top and a canal below.

The walkway along the canal is dark and wet, rarely getting sunshine in the narrow chasm of sheer rock that still shows the rough gouges from the iron and muscle that created a path for the water and canal boats to pass through the city and to the sea.

The city has somehow managed to keep the rock clear of the ubiquitous graffiti found on every flat surface in the world, or perhaps the green slime growing on the slick rock is deterrent enough.

A family played cards on the deck of a canal boat moored just outside the narrow opening where the city came down to meet the canal. They were renting the "narrow boat" and touring the canals of Cheshire, drinking and playing cards along the way.

Given the choice I would have enjoyed a slow drift along the canals, but my travels took me back to work, this time ten miles east of Chester, to a little community called St David's just inside the Welsh border.

The town itself is actually called Ewloe, but the hotel/resort seems to have taken over the identity of the area. St David's consists of some office buildings, the hotel, and a couple of pubs. It feels very new and clean, with only the traffic signs telling me I was in Wales by warning me that my speed would be checked by a *camerâu cyflymder*.

The Victory pub was located in the hotel, the walls covered with pictures announcing "Victory" combed from the Internet and novelty shops sporting Winston Churchill, football stars and a WWII Dalek.

It very much reminded me of the pubs refurbished by aliens in *The World's End*. Too clean, too nice, too much the vision of what a "pub" is "supposed to be" the way TGI Friday's tries to be festive. But they had proper cask ale, so that's alright.

As I sat in the nearly empty pub under the Victory posters while a Fresh Prince of Bel Aire video played on the main screen and European football and cricket played on the other screens, I overheard the conversation about "the trouble with America" from a couple of tables down.

A small group of women and men were well into their third round and one of the middle-aged women was complaining about how her son really wanted to go to America. Not being the shy type, I picked up my pint, wandered down to their table and introduced myself.

"Hi. I'm the American."

There was an almost, but not quite, uncomfortable moment while they worked out that I wasn't offended at all, and soon I was standing the fourth round while talking about the grand American landscape and how, yes Alabama really is like that, but there's a lot more to the U.S. than rednecks and McDonald's.

Every now and then the blonde sitting across from me would screw up a bit of focus through her gin and tonic soaked Sunday and ask her friends, "I'm sorry, who is this?" And they would again explain I was the American.

"Oh. Right... but who is he again?"

We chatted about entertainment as an export and that not all Americans are buffoonish or warmongers, and for the next couple of days I had dinner companions as I kept running into them and they would wave me over to join them.

I have to admit I usually obscure, if not actually hide, my Americanisms on most of my European trips. We aren't really the most liked people on the planet right now; while I've been asked if I'm from Ireland or Australia and I don't lie about my homeland, it's sometimes better to not be the American.

But, for some reason, in Northern England I embraced my American roots. I'm only English if you ignore the three hundred and some-odd years since John Bissell sailed to the Colonies in the 1600's. I'm more Native American than English by direct lineage, my great-grandmother having been full-blooded Cherokee.

And being the American worked out well for me in places like Manchester and Ewloe. Traveling for business meant I wasn't really in the tourist centers except for my side trip to Chester. There was a sense of pity for my plight being so far from home, and there was a bit of curiosity -- they don't get a lot of

Americans hanging out in pubs in Ewloe which made me a bit exotic.

Who would have thought I could have been exotic in a small town in Wales?

English Dancing in the English Countryside

THE GREY HAIRED QUARTET OF FIDDLES, CONCERTINA AND flute played an old tune in waltz time in a small village somewhere between Liverpool and Manchester as I reminded my partner, "Right hand..." I think the other dancers were surprised not only that an American had randomly turned up at their local dance, but maybe a bit more that I could actually dance.

I had learned to dance in Cincinnati. When contra dancing wasn't enough, I found the vintage ballroom dance group. It was like contra had been a gateway drug as ballroom soon led to English Country. And while I hadn't been to an English dance in years, I figured, if I'm in the English countryside there should be an English Country Dance and Google didn't disappoint.

I finished meetings in St Davids and took an early afternoon train from Chester. A change of trains in Liverpool and then that odd bit of track in Kirkby where I had to get off the train, walk through an arch in the old, crumbling, brick wall that blocked the rail and get on the next train, and I was soon in Rainford.

Well, I was actually a mile and a half outside the village on a platform bordered by old brownish-black brick and rock walls with a gate that led to a trail along an old right of way that went to the village.

The trees lining the walk rustled in the June breeze and occasionally gave way to views of the green fields beyond. I found the theme from *Vicar of Dibley* running through my head as I walked through the English countryside hoping that I wasn't wandering into a town like Royston Vasey from *The League of*

Gentlemen; even when in a real place I find television framing my reference...

But, then, often I find those stereotypes from TV exist because they are a perfect match for the real place. Three old locals, including the proprietor, sat at the bar in the pub, which was traditional brown wood wainscoting and dull paisley wallpapered walls covered with paintings of people from centuries gone by. There were flowers in the windows and dining tables scattered about in the sitting room; this was a proper, local pub in the village, not a dive bar like we seem to always have in small U.S. towns.

I ordered the roast and a dark ale. When the meal came the waitress set it up on a table and came to fetch me from the bar -- it was implied that no one, not even a lone American, eats a proper meal at the bar.

Thick black gravy filled the bottom of the plate and glazed the beef roast with a dark shine. The bowl of hand-mashed potatoes sat next to the bowl of steamed or parboiled carrots. If you believe the food in England is overcooked canned salt, your information is probably forty years out of date -- I wouldn't judge U.S. cuisine by the 1970s either.

After my early dinner I walked around the village. The sign in the church graveyard gave the service times for Sunday, a "tot's service" on Wednesday mornings, and something called "Shopper's Communion" which I think has more to do with, "Come check out our church" and less to do with ladies with bags marked Gucci popping in for a quick shot of the blood of Christ on a Thursday morning.

Behind the church was a cricket field with young men in white uniforms scattered around the field while the runners hit the ball and ran back and forth. The parents sat in their cars reading or listening to the radio; apparently even practice matches are too long to hold anyone's attention even in Rainford Village.

I finally made my way to Rainford Hall and found myself in a surprisingly familiar place: a dance in an old building with a room that could be an auditorium or a basketball court with aging folkies trying to keep the old dances alive. Many of the same characters were there that I knew from dancing in the U.S. -- the charismatic bandleader, the harried dance organizer, the ditzy dancer who forgets how to dance halfway through a set...

They served tea and biscuits at the break; not the fancy tea settings I had seen in Manchester, but the same sort of spread that we did in the grange hall in Portland. There were store-bought biscuits and someone brought a cake and everyone pitched in to clean up before we went into the second half of the dance.

Of course, there were things about the hall that were decidedly British, like the old photo of Winston Churchill on one side of the band and a young Queen on the other and in one corner I found a framed sheet of paper typed on an old typewriter that was probably new when it was written that told the story about how the Earl of Derby had graciously donated the land for the Hall in the late 1800s.

I knew the familiar tunes and at least one or two of the dances -- there were American contra dances and English dances in equal measure. They finished with a big circle dance singing, "Oh Dem Golden Slippers" which the dance organizer seemed apologetic to me about.

I never knew the history of that song or that it was performed in blackface, and I certainly didn't think that my hosts might think I could be touchy about their referencing my country's racism. I'm sure if I had figured it out at the time I would have returned the potential mild offense by laughing and saying, "You think THAT'S racist? You have no idea..."

I got a ride to my hotel from one of the musicians and his wife. We chatted about how they had promoted English Country dancing when that Colin Firth series was popular by advertising,

"Learn to dance like in *Pride and Prejudice*" only that no one really stayed after a few dances. I had been lucky to find them in a hall as they had been holding "house dances" until this event -- clear the living room furniture out of the way and make room for a very short set.

The next day I got on a train which took me to a plane which took me to another airport and I got on another plane for the grueling ten hours over Greenland and Canada to get home. That night I visited my local pub and hassled the bar manager for proper cask conditioned ale.

After a couple weeks of soft, warm, English ale I found that our cold, carbonated Northwest beers were painful going down with the hard bubbles scraping the esophagus and then building up in the stomach. And no Sunday roast...

Where London had surprised me with its melting pot of languages and cultures, Merseyside and Manchester counties fulfilled my fantasies of what the "real England" is like. Could I live in that part of the world? Probably, but I know that I was lucky to see it in late May and early June when the countryside is perfect and everyone is mellow.

I'll need to go back in February and see how the mood is when everyone is light-deprived and trapped indoors.

The Nordic Experience

I was stuck in Amsterdam on a 23-hour layover when a glass door opened across the way. A deep, female voice called out, "Hey you! C'mere! I want to shag you!"

The woman selling her product saw me a reasonable customer and was simply presenting her wares. A lone, middle-aged white guy wandering the streets of the red light district could only want one thing, after all. Except I wasn't actually interested in spending €50 for a quick cuddle and a tug at the prostitute automat.

But it was only polite to saunter over to politely decline as she asked me if I wanted some Jamaican Loving.

"Oh, are you from Jamaica?" I asked.

Noticing my American accent she suddenly got a little less sure of herself and her backstory. Somehow Jamaica is closer to the U.S. or maybe she just realized I wasn't a Londoner on a day trip, changing her assessment of my expectations.

"Well, my father was, but I was born here..."

We chatted about the Islands and America for a few minutes and I told her I wasn't really interested in any services, but I did ask her if there was a decent place for lunch nearby. Apparently the Argentinean barbeque in Amsterdam is amazing, and she gave me directions over the canal and down the street telling me to have a nice stay and waving bye to me around her closing door as I went to find lunch.

Norway

THE SEA WAS BOILING. IT HAD BEEN A LITTLE ABOVE FREEZING the day before, but by the time I walked out of my hotel on a sunny day that threatened frostbite the temperature had dropped to well below freezing, and a bit more. Where the cold air touched the warm sea a layer of frothy, ice-cold steam clung to the waves.

Fortunately there is always an H&M nearby and I was able to buy a sock cap to cover my ears which felt like they were going to shatter in the cold. If I thought I was being an American wuss, the cold was confirmed when a local walked in the door and said in English, "Damn, it's cold out there!"

I slung my messenger bag over my shoulder and headed to the client's office on the top of the hill. At one point an old man called to me in Norwegian and I, almost embarrassedly, explained I only spoke English. He switched to English and asked if I could help him across the frozen street that couldn't have been slicker if a Zamboni had smoothed it.

When I told him I didn't think I was much more stable than him he said, "Everyone is more stable than me!" and grabbed my arm. Fortunately he was right, and we made it across safely to the graveled sidewalk.

We were passed by lean, Nordic men and women in spandex out for their morning run as we hobbled across the icy street. Maybe running makes you more stable and you can adjust for slipping from step to step but, really, I have no idea how they kept their footing at a full run over the ice even with studs in the soles of their shoes.

I climbed the hill and had a few bad moments where I really thought there was no way to go unless I crawled, but the kids and mothers with babies seemed to be doing fine, so I continued and managed to make it to the top without breaking my ego or bones.

When I met the client and they realized I had walked there was a pause. "You're American, right?"

"Yes..." I slowly responded.

"But Americans never walk! Were you okay?"

This wasn't the ribbing country folk give city folk, this was sincere concern about my ability to navigate the snow and ice. I told them about the Puget Sound and the Cascades and how much Trondheim's fjords and mountains reminded me of where I live, and they seemed to settle down a bit. A bit.

The day went like many other days in my job. We went to a windowless conference room and I walked through my presentation. We had lunch in the company cafeteria, although I have to admit most corporate cafeterias don't serve reindeer meatballs or have a panoramic view of snowcovered mountains and the sea.

During the day there were the standard questions for me in English and the expected side discussions among the client's team in Norwegian. The trouble with Norwegian is how much English has stolen from it. You almost feel like you can understand it, the way you almost feel like you're tracking a conversation when you're stoned. The words fall by you and you grasp at them like phantom butterflies, never quite catching the meaning even if you can follow the mood.

During a break the woman who led the group was chatting with a few tech guys while I responded to emails. The words flowed by sounding like "Fuder ein to lenderberry ven two girls one cup derfur doodle oven."

My head snapped up and I said, "Um... Sorry? You know I don't speak Norwegian but... are you talking about what I think you're talking about?"

She gave me an embarrassed grin and we went on to have the conversation that always follows the phrase, "Two girls, one cup," where no one who had seen the video would discuss what was in it and those who had seen it begged to be enlightened. I honestly don't know if everyone was speaking English or Norwegian at that point, the script is just too well set and we all played our parts.

Later we had dinner at a tapas restaurant in the town center. Rioja and small plates while the temperature continued to plummet and ice formed on the windows. After dinner a group of us went downstairs to the pub in the lower level of the old building in the thousand-year-old village. A fire burned in the corner of the low-ceilinged room that was clad in the dark varnished wood that seems universal in old taverns in Europe.

As I chatted about what to drink with the bartender we played the game that all experts play with each other. As an expert in all things alcoholic, or at least the many things I have poured down my gullet over the years, I upped the ante by talking about the beers and drinks I knew and he saw and raised those drinks with his own experience. My Cascade cred went a long ways, his Belgian knowledge was enlightening, but my brewer relative and personal experience broke the bank.

He did one of those things that only very earnest people, or used car salesmen, do. He leaned in, lowered his voice and said, "I can't believe I'm actually offering this, I only have three bottles left, but..." and pulled out a Thomas Hardy's Ale with a serial number on it (05731 if anyone is counting). The brewery had closed four years before, so to say, "I only have three bottles" is to say, "I only have three bottles." There will be no more.

I looked at it, I looked at him. I looked at it again, and in an equally hushed voice, "How much are you getting for that?"

"Three hundred krone."

Quick math... Move the decimal point over one place... round up about 20-25%... Forty bucks. For a 250ml bottle of beer. Barely over a cup, which made it just about five dollars an ounce... And so worth it.

I sat in the dark room with sheets of ice flowing by outside on the river and I cradled my glass, warming the beer, letting it breathe, letting it change as I worked my way through it sip by sip. My Norwegian clients and even my colleague from London scoffed at the American who spent so much for an English ale in Norway.

But there are those moments. Moments where you are in a cellar pub watching the ice drift by on the Nidelva while the logs in the corner hearth slowly turn from fire to coals and you know, this moment will never happen again. If this wasn't one of those moments I don't know that I would ever recognize one.

I strolled back to my hotel around two in the morning, when the chill of night was probably the coldest it could be, but the warmth of the English ale and the Norwegian hospitality kept the ice at bay while the stars twinkled above the snow-covered rooftops.

Soon I was done with business in Trondheim, but I took a couple of extra days in Norway. I had planned to take the train to Oslo through the mountains, only to discover there was a school holiday and the ticket counter told me there were no seats on the mountain train. I could take the coastal route, which would be longer and not nearly as interesting, but Lillehammer was out.

So I played the brash American card and asked if the conductor might have a different answer. The woman at the ticket counter seemed a little surprised that I would even think of such a thing, but said I could always ask.

It was barely dawn and the platform was cluttered with families and ski gear returning to southern parts of Norway as the train started boarding. Suddenly it was a chaos with skis and children all going different directions. I found a conductor and showed him my ticket that I had bought online before leaving Portland and asked if there was room on the train. He barely glanced at me and pointed me to a car.

The soaring mountains along the train route are deceiving. This is the same mountain range where the bluegrass music I learned to contra dance to was invented, only this part of the chain broke apart from the Appalachia millions of years ago leaving scattered bits in Scotland and Iceland. While some parts of Norway climb to respectable heights, this weathered old chain of mountains is practically sea level.

Sea level or not, the snow lies thick on the ground and when a lake comes into view it is an open plain of solid white. The low sun in February doesn't quite clear the tops of the mountains and makes the small towns and villages along the way seem cozier with the warm lights coming from the houses on the hills.

The electric train slipped through mountain valleys as I chatted online with Markie over the free WiFi, sending pictures home to her as she was just crawling into bed in the previous night, nine hours in my past and over six thousand miles away.

Lunch in the dining car was much like lunch in the dining car of the Amtrak that runs between Eugene and Seattle, although the tea was much better and the beer was much more expensive. Soon the wild Norway outside my window was replaced with a more developed Norway, and new tracks and overhead wires came together as we closed in on Oslo and the ride began to feel more like a commuter train. Then the walls climbed out of the snowy fields and the train went underground.

I dragged my suitcase through the ice and slush in the dark late afternoon of Oslo in February. Trondheim is the third largest city in Norway, but it is still a small town. Oslo is definitely the big city with tall buildings, heavy traffic and the noise that goes with it. Arriving from underground made the transition from Nordic village to urban Scandinavia that much more striking.

The Radisson Blu was 34 stories, maybe a bit more with the outside deck of the rooftop bar that wouldn't be open until the days became much longer and warmer. My room was on the 28th floor; unlike the small room in Trondheim, this room reminded me of the suites at the Venetian in Las Vegas with a large sitting area and king-size bed that faced the floor-to-ceiling windows where Oslo was spread out beneath me.

167 | Mundane Journeys

That night I went to the part of the bar on the 34th floor that is open in February (the indoor part, that is) and told the bartender I like "strong drinks with a lot of herbaceousness." He asked if I trusted him, which kind of forced me to say yes. He then proceeded to make what he called a "Norwegian Sazerac" made with Aquavit, Aperol and a few secret ingredients. No matter what was in it it was perfect to sip while looking out over the lights of the twisting streets of Oslo from way on high.

Soon I was chatting with a somewhat grizzled man who said the last time he had seen this view it was from the box of a crane; he had helped build the place we were lounging in and wanted to see it again, although the ambiance and liquor were much better this time around.

He had learned a lot of his English from Irish ironworkers and his stories of building skyscrapers, chasing women and drinking were liberally soaked with enough profanity I finally understood the phrase "make a sailor blush." I'm not a shrinking violet but "colorful" would be an adjective to describe his language only if you compared it to what you see in the toilet after throwing up a night's heavy drink and food.

The next day I had breakfast in the hotel before heading out to explore. Scandinavian breakfasts are a vegan's nightmare with the cold cuts, cheeses and pickled fish. Fortunately I'm not a vegan and I'm in heaven. I load my plate with meat and fish and while I try to balance the heavy, fatty food with a bowl of fruit and yogurt, the yogurt is often more like kiefer and the fruit often includes lingonberries that are more jam than fruit.

The fact that the orange juice is labeled "appelsinjuice" and the apple juice is "eplejuice" is a bit confusing at first, but orange is orange which solves any question quickly enough. And the coffee is real. I've been told that if you ask for decaf in Norway you will get honest blank looks; it simply doesn't exist. Strong coffee is probably the only thing that keeps the economy moving when daylight drops to little more than five hours in the winter.

Google Maps had pointed me toward the Royal Palace and the Nobel Peace Center, so I pulled on my H&M beanie from Trondheim and my wool pea coat from Freddie's in Portland successfully creating a combo that made me look like an AWOL sailor, and I headed out into the cold, February day.

There's something wrong about a TGI Friday's next to an ancient cathedral, but there it was. And a Burger King... Of course the Oslo Cathedral was at the beginning of the main shopping district which was one of those open-air streets that doesn't allow cars, that Europeans favor and American's don't seem to understand.

Someone had built a six-foot-tall replica of the Cathedral out of snow on the walkway by the actual Cathedral. It wasn't perfect but it was impressive with snow towers and snow buttresses and a turret that was inexplicably a man in a top hat. There was a tin can in front of the snow cathedral with a few krone in it -- I don't know if it was the person who built the snow sculpture or an enterprising homeless person cashing in on the tourists, so I just took a picture and continued toward the palace.

Soon I came to the broad parade area at the Royal Palace of the King of Norway. Two guards stood at attention at either side of the front door and a couple more marched in an exaggerated stride along the front of the Palace.

There were no fences or gates, and I could walk right up to the front door if I wanted, which is kept open in the summertime, although I had been told at the hotel that I would be stopped by one of the festively dressed guards if I tried to actually go in.

A block or so away was the U.S. Embassy with its concrete posts on the sidewalk to prevent a vehicle from getting to the heavy, steel fence which surrounded a "kill-zone" cement perimeter of the concrete building with narrow windows that looked like arrow slits in a medieval castle. Armed guards stood inside the double gates of the pedestrian entrance. This is how we present ourselves to an ally in a peaceful city.

And it's not just a peaceful city, Oslo is home to the Nobel Peace Center, a fact apparently lost on the American delegation. I left the barricaded compound behind and wandered along the quiet streets down to the harbor where sheets of ice and ships with tall masts floated silently in the water.

In the Nobel Center I found a huge exhibit on the President of the United States of America, which seemed a bit ironic in 2013 as the debate over his executive drone strikes and unilateral military action was beginning to get louder.

I think Obama got the Nobel Peace Prize in 2009 because it was just such a relief not to have Bush and Cheney telling the rest of the world that we have the biggest army and the most guns. Even if Obama has proved to be the leader of the country with the most powerful military on Earth, they still really seemed to like him at the Peace Center, equating him with Martin Luther King Jr. in a number of exhibits, suggesting an end to racism in America.

The medieval Akershus Fortress overlooks the harbor and the Peace Center, a reminder that Norway hasn't always been a quiet, peaceful place. I walked up the hill and through an ancient arch in a wall built from giant rocks in a time before tractors or boom cranes.

Down a narrow path I found piles of treasure shining in a glass-enclosed alcove in an old wall -- I never found out if it was an art installation, national treasure or if it was a rift in reality and I was looking in on the land of Faerie.

I climbed the gravel path through the cold fog that shrouded the castle walls, giving the place an even more medieval look. Torchlight flickered from woven metal stakes along the path, although the flame itself was from a giant tea light like the ones they sell at IKEA (and may well have been from there with the birthplace of IKEA only three hundred miles away).

Under the stone arch ahead I saw soldiers, not in formal costume but in olive green and carrying submachine guns. Some kind of formal event was going on in the old castle and I heard rumor that the King of Norway was in attendance; perhaps the friendly, open-door Palace was misleading. Royalty in the 21st century still needs a real military, not just men in fancy dress.

Rather than heading into the thick of a military force, I turned toward the top of the wall and found the Norwegian Resistance museum. The museum was in an old building built on top of an older wall, and as I descended through the exhibits the brick gave way to large masonry formed by the giant rocks of the medieval walls. It seemed appropriate that the walls became more dungeon-like as the history grew darker with how bad things had been under Hitler and how Norway fought as best it could even after being conquered.

I soon left the Middle Ages and headed to the future by way of the Oslo Opera House. The building lifts out of the Oslofjord like the sheets of ice jutting from the water. The angled roofline comes all the way down to the pedestrian walkway along the water, and, despite the icy conditions and the signs warning people to stay off the roof, the roof was crawling with Norwegians. I personally didn't trust my balance or my footwear enough to risk the climb and instead walked the perimeter of the Opera House peering into the costume shop at naked mannequins and the coffee shop with clothed visitors.

Out in the frozen fjord sat a ghost ship; the artist's intention amplified by the ice and fog wrapping the ship in a dreamlike haze of winter. I took a picture of myself reflected in the glass surface of the Opera House with the ghost ship behind me; the refraction of the reflection gave my image a similar, ghostly appearance that was somewhat unsettling.

Bundled in my pea coat and beanie, the combination of my AWOL sailor look and the odd lighting effect gave the impression of a lonely spirit wandering the seas forever, not really knowing he is a ghost. And when traveling alone in a foreign city, I sometimes feel like a ghost trapped just outside the world of the living, unable to speak the language or understand what is really going on.

The short northern daylight was coming to an end as I hiked back up to the hotel, passing the TGI Fridays and Burger King, but finding a local restaurant that served Nøgne Ø beer, which wasn't honestly that great, but it was decidedly Norwegian so it was good in the moment.

Finally the time came to crawl back down into the rail station and take the not-so-secret tunnel out of the city to the airport. I had a 23-hour layover ahead of me in Amsterdam, and then the ten hour flight home to Portland where winters aren't nearly as cold and the history isn't as cluttered.

Sweden

I LEFT PORTLAND AT NOON IN A LIGHT DRIZZLE AND LANDED in Stockholm at noon in a light drizzle. I later compared the two pictures I had taken out the window from the beginning and end of my trip. The view of the wing and the tarmac and the baggage carts looked almost identical and other than the KLM logo replacing the Delta logo, it was hard to tell which airport was which.

This was around the time the Northeast US was stuck in the polar vortex -- it was 20 below in Chicago and somewhere in the 40s in Stockholm. I had expected ice and snow like I had found in Norway the year before, but I was instead greeted by exactly the weather I had left thousands of miles away.

As the taxi drove past shopping malls and car dealerships with embankments of wet, brown grass and thin stands of fir trees, it felt even more like the Pacific Northwest. Later in the day I went for a hike along trails in the woods while runners carrying ski poles trained for a cross-country ski race that might be canceled and mountain bikers pushed through an old cyclocross course in the muddy forest.

I sometimes think humans are terraforming Earth, except I think of it as Euroforming. We make everywhere we go more like Europe with European plants and architecture and food. You can call it Ameriforming if you want, but we Americans are just better at it because we were the original Euroformers -- our heroes include Johnny Appleseed spreading European apples across North America and the pioneers "clearing the land and planting wheat."

Most of our Euroforming today is in the cities. I was somewhat surprised to find 7-Elevens in Tokyo and Domino's Pizza in Iceland, but not really. We expect our global brands to be global. I like to believe, though, that when you get out of the cities you get to see how things are different, with landscapes and vegetation that stun you with their foreignness, but things weren't that different.

Even without humans giving plants new homes in faraway places, this wasn't really as far away as all that. Sweden is farther north than Oregon, but both places have short days in winter and long days in summer. Both places have oceans and mountains. And, although a bit farther from Portland, both connect to the Arctic Ice so plants and animals might not have always needed to hitch a lift with a homesick Viking.

The land outside the suburbs of Stockholm felt like home, with the trees and grasses and muddy trails and the suburban town of Kista, with its buildings built in the last hundred years, just like the cities of the Northwest... didn't feel anything like home.

If I could catalog all the differences between downtown Portland and downtown Kista my list wouldn't be able to explain what makes Kista a foreign city because too much of it was too subtle to register as I walked down the street, but was just visible enough to give me that feeling of foreignness.

The traffic lights are a little different. The signs for companies are placed in odd places a few stories above the street. There are Toyotas and Volvos, but there are also Skodas and Citrons. The kids on skateboards dressed like kids on skateboards, but they wait patiently at the streetlight for the signal, regardless of the traffic.

As I approached the front desk at the Memory Hotel I was greeted by a woman speaking a cheery stream syllables that must have been Swedish but sounded more like Russian than the stuff the Swedish Chef from *The Muppets* spoke (in fact, Norwegian sounds more like the Swedish Chef than Swedish does). I responded with "Good evening" or something equally obviously in English and she shifted seamlessly. There was the usual problem with my credit card because American banks don't do chips right but we made it work, and she handed me my room key.

What she handed me was a punch card made of plastic. It went into the lock the same way modern key cards with magnetic strips work, except this was entirely mechanical. Push it in, feel the pins inside the lock sliding over the bumps and into holes, and then push the handle down. Jiggle the key a bit, try again, and the door opens.

There was no flashing light or buzz -- it was as if the key had been made in the Middle Ages by a time traveler who had visited the 1970s and was mimicking the tech as best he could. I assume the Memory Hotel and its retro-future tech key were remnants of when Ericsson was on the cutting edge and Kista was the new tech hub in the days of tubes and coils.

Sometimes the subtler differences are more striking than an in-your-face foreign experience. Around the time my card-punched room key was being invented a Japanese roboticist named Masahiro Mori coined the phrase "The Uncanny Valley" to describe how an android that looks almost human, but not quite, is creepy, while R2-D2 is cute.

Maybe it was the jet lag, maybe the unexpected weather, but that first day I found suburban Sweden in that uncanny valley. It was too close to normal to be normal.

The snow came the next day and the world became slippery and things started to feel more like the Sweden I expected. I walked to the client's office, got the grainy photo badge that I never actually wore, and sat in a windowless conference room with a couple of Swedes and an Indian. If you want any indication of how the global economy is changing just look at any tech team in the world -- there may or may not be an American, but there will always be an Indian.

Lunch the first day was in the corporate cafeteria; I remember hearing that when Norwegians and Swedes visit places like Minnesota they try to be polite about the "traditional foods."

But the foods you find at an average American Scandinavian Festival are what the peasants brought along a couple hundred years ago. Even a corporate cafe has better food than Minnesotan peasant food.

I took the train into Stockholm that night, getting from the office to the platform with a short walk through the shopping mall, over a pedestrian bridge, and past the Romanies who could have pulled their wardrobe from a 1930s gypsy film, with the hats and scarves. They sat or stood along the sides of the walkway, talking among themselves, hardly noticing my passing. I had expected some kind of panhandling or hustle from them, but this seemed to just be the place they were hanging out and I wasn't part of their world.

The electric commuter train raced along an elevated track past the woods I had hiked through and then it plunged underground. Each station was decorated differently, some with bright colors others with the natural grey color of the shock-crete that was spayed on the roughly-hewn rock walls. The platforms in Stockholm are the only subway platforms where I have felt really underground because they left the walls looking like a cave wall after the diggers had hauled away the debris. No shiny tile of the Underground in London, no perfect tubes of the Metro in Washington D.C.

Eventually I came out of the tunnel system and into another European city. There is a point when you spend your days flying from iconic city to iconic city that the icons begin to get fuzzy. Coming out of the train station was like coming out of train stations everywhere -- the crowds push past the animated advertising kiosks in the entry area, queue up for the escalator, and come into a brightly-lit shopping area with the usual suspects like H&M and Nike housed in modern buildings on an old town square.

Yes, the advertising was in Swedish including an animation of David Hasselhoff's *Baywatch* pecs flexing, but if I remember the shopping center around the Lime Street station in Liverpool and compare it in my mind to the shopping center around the T-Centralen station in Stockholm I find the details become fuzzy and fuse together.

When I was in Oslo and visited the Nobel Peace Center I told myself I would visit the Nobel Museum in Stockholm someday. And now that I was here, I completely forgot about the Nobel Center, and while my random walking often takes me amazing places, I probably walked about a block away from the Museum without ever knowing it was there.

The open flame of oil lamps was inviting as I walked by a small restaurant with an indecipherable menu. They got me settled in a cozy corner by the window that looked out onto the narrow, cobbled alleyway -- if you suffer from light deprivation depression, I don't recommend Scandinavian countries in February. But if, like me, you like low lighting and walkways lit by torches and candles, it's the perfect place to be.

When the waiter realized I couldn't read the menu he pulled an enormous board out of the corner where they had translated the day's menu into English. The small restaurant became even smaller with a six foot tall partition between me and the other patrons, and I quickly settled on the elk.

Of course, translations don't always translate well. My experience of elk comes from the Pacific Northwest where elk are like large deer. Elk in Sweden turns out to be moose. Probably for the best I didn't know that as I would have otherwise been thinking of the intro to *Monty Python and the Holy Grail* with the "majestik møose" and thus avoided giggling to myself in the corner.

But whatever large ungulate the steak had come from, it was perfect, as were so many meals in this part of the world.

While I was on this trip my company was releasing a series of technical videos I had filmed over the previous few months. One of the challenges with describing technology is how quickly things change and videos go out of date, so I decided to solve this by recording a brief intro for each week to point out that, yes, I know things have changed and, more importantly, here's where to look for new stuff.

The fact I was booked solid in different cities around the world was just coincidence, but it let me film in Sweden one week and Denver the next. Finding a backdrop to prove I really was in these places wasn't as tricky as actually setting up my laptop and microphone outdoors.

On my last day in Stockholm I took the train into town again and walked out to Skeppsholmen Island in the early morning. This was tourist picture-perfect Stockholm with none of that "uncanny valley." The Old World feeling was impossible to miss as I came around the east end of the Island, past the old tall-masted ship, along the walk with the bronze statues next to the low brick buildings painted yellow and with everything wrapped in a light blanket of snow.

And there, across a small bay on a tiny island, was the red brick of Kastellholmen tucked into the hillside, surrounded by giant leafless trees. The tourists hadn't come out on this early, snowy morning and I was able to position my laptop on a park bench, putting my rain jacket on the ground so I could sit down in the line of the camera with the small castle in the frame behind me.

They say public speaking is everyone's biggest fear, but I felt much more nervous sitting on the ground facing a park bench talking to my laptop with no one around. Occasionally I would see a runner approaching or a couple would come walking by and I would stop recording and play with the controls of my laptop.

But no one called the police or stood and pointed at the funny man sitting in the snow, and I was able to get my video recorded. I tucked my laptop back into my briefcase, slid my wet rain jacket into the strap to let it dry, and quietly slipped away.

With my headphones on and mouse in hand, I edited my video presentation in a coffee shop in the Moderna Museet. My nervousness about being a spectacle in the snow passed as I sipped a cappuccino at a high table with the clean lines one would expect not only in a Swedish coffee shop, but are almost required in a modern art museum.

After uploading the final recording so someone in San Jose could worry about publishing it when the Earth got around to showing them the sunrise in six or seven hours, I packed up and went exploring.

The one thing the locals had told me I was required to see was the old ship at the Vasa Museum. The masts stuck out of the museum building just across the water and beside it were the towers of some amusement park, which apparently wasn't amusing in February as it looked abandoned in the winter snow.

The Vasa was an amazing work of reclamation. The huge wooden warship had sunk on its maiden voyage as it barely left port, being a little top heavy when it fired a triumphant cannon salute the ship rocked too far to one side, caught the wind and rocked too far back.

The John Hartford song "In Plain View of Town" came to mind. In the song a riverboat ran the barges aground:

> *Looks like no matter, how hard they push,*
> *These barges are still on the ground*
> *Must have been embarrassing for the pilot*
> *Here in plain view of the town*

Somehow I don't think getting a barge stuck on a sandbar came close to the entire ship sinking to the bottom of the harbor in plain view of town. And she laid there for over three hundred years in the dark, cold harbor mud.

When they pulled the ship out of the muddy, briny deep in the 1960s it wasn't as simple as putting it in a museum -- they had to spray it with water for years as they renovated it so it wouldn't dry up and blow away as rotten wood dust.

Then they sprayed it with polyethylene glycol for another seventeen years, slowly replacing the water with plastic, reminding me of the plasticization of cadavers. Yes, the ship may last another four hundred years, but in a weirdly preserved state like something from an old Vincent Price film.

Terraces rise up on all sides of the ship letting you look down on the decks from above, peer in through the gun ports, and walk beneath the bulk of the hull. And down there, on the ground level of what was once the bottom of a dry-dock, are the skeletons.

Sailors who were trapped in the ship as it sank, some drowning, some crushed under cannons, and whose bones rested in the muddy seawater for 333 years, are now laid out under glass for the curious to gawk at. From a scientific standpoint it's fascinating, even if it is a bit macabre. But perhaps any preservation is a form of necromancy -- raising the dead for our viewing pleasure.

The snow was still on the ground when I came out of the darkened museum but the ice had begun to melt and the walkways were clear as I wandered through the park and along the water where ducks used the ice shelves as bathing platforms, dipping their bills into the water over the edge of the half-submerged sheet of ice they stood on.

Then I slipped into fairyland for a moment when I turned a corner to find what looked like a small Russian castle. I never found out what the turret or the industrial grade brick smokestack were for originally, but the spiral pattern up the smokestack topped with the metalwork made it look like Rapunzel's tower, other than only being three stories high.

Slipping in the small door at the bottom of the smokestack I found a little cafe with a fireplace and a counter piled with cakes and pastries while the sound of whistling steam frothing milk promised a cappuccino.

As I surveyed the plenty, a woman holding a baby said something in Swedish to me as she held her glass under a water spigot which she could obviously not turn with her hands full. I turned the spigot and filled her glass, she smiled and said "Tack" which was maybe the one Swedish word I did understand, and went back to her table.

After I ordered my äppelkaka and cappuccino she came up to me and apologized for speaking Swedish to me because she heard me ordering in English. Why she had to apologize to me for speaking her native language in her native country never has made sense to me. Besides, women with babies have some sort of universal language and are always understood. Or at least should be.

I had an early morning flight the next day, made more stressful by being dropped at the wrong KLM terminal and having to power walk and run the length of the Arlanda airport only to find my flight delayed by the twenty minutes I had lost. Then I played "Find the American" in the waiting area (hint: it was the guy in sweatpants talking loudly about sales) as I slipped out of the quiet, polite and sometimes weird world of Scandinavia and back into the mundane world of airplanes and terminals.

Iceland

THE GREAT ICE FIELDS WERE SPREAD OUT AROUND ME WITH the sky a churning texture of grey and glowing clouds overhead as I piloted my Toyota Yaris deeper into the Icelandic wilderness. I found myself channeling Jeremy Clarkson of *Top Gear*, talking to a nonexistent camera near the passenger seat.

"I'm braving the wilderness of Iceland... In a YARIS!"

The Yaris was the cheapest car at the rental. With the front-wheel drive turning 14" wheels, a windshield that only needed one wiper arm, and barely room for my messenger bag in the back, it is a perfect runabout in places like Tokyo or London. Exactly the kind of car you don't drive into the frozen wastes a hundred miles from the Arctic Circle.

I had learned to drive on the wet, winding roads of the North Coast in California in a Datsun 1200, a rear-wheel-drive car with far less power and comfort than the Yaris. And I'm no stranger to mountainous country, having learned what the ice feels like beneath my wheels, when to let the ice take me, and when to apply power to get out of it.

In front of me a Land Rover slipped and slid back and forth on the frozen road surface, undoubtedly driven by British tourists who felt they were safe by renting a four-wheel-drive SUV built by their countrymen, not realizing that it takes more than a big car to drive safely on snow and ice.

I decided it was best to let them have their own bit of road before they had a chance to spin around and smash into my tiny commuter car with their heavily armored assault vehicle, so I found a turnout where Icelandic ponies lined up by the fence waiting for their alfalfa dole.

These little horses somehow survive the dead of winter with nothing but their scraggly coats. They stood together, some lying on the frozen ground, staring off into the distance without really seeing anything as they waited for food and waited for spring. The joy I felt of the end of winter in the Midwest probably wouldn't even register on the pony joy scale with what they must feel when the ice finally melts and the sun returns and life blooms again in Iceland.

I continued along the Golden Circle, the touristy drive through rocky fields of lava and the geysers at Geiser, not to be confused with the hotel I stayed at with my dad impossibly far away, but pronounced the way he joked about it being for old folks.

You may be able to brag about standing with one foot on either side of the Continental Divide or that you stood on the Four Corners and were in four states simultaneously. But I can say I drove from North America to Europe that day -- the lava and the geysers and the hot springs are formed by the rift below Iceland where the North American and European plates meet.

Some people dive into the waters that fill a crack between the plates and put their hands on both continents at once. I just rumbled over a bit of asphalt by a marker with less vibration than tires on a cattle guard and thought to myself, "Huh... was that a sign for Europe?"

Although it is a very real geological line it still feels very imaginary like many lines in the world -- the rocky fields look the same on either continental shelf that were covered by the same lava, and the ponies and snow don't know that they are crossing from one continent to another.

Eventually I found myself in an icy parking area slipping my tiny car into a spot by buses and vans and poorly parked Land Rovers. The crowds formed a straggling line as they walked away from the cars along a dirty bit of snow, making them look like a line of ants heading toward a sugar cube. I dutifully joined in not knowing what was over the ridge.

I have never been to the Grand Canyon, and I think I might be a bit disappointed now that I have seen the Gullfoss. The giant river falling down the cliff face would be amazing enough in the summer, but in March the cliffs were made of rock and ice that looked like a layer cake made from mashed potatoes and sugar.

Icicles the size of church spires clung to the rock, overlapping and cutting into each other looking more like a frozen waterfall the closer they got to the water far below. I could see layers of snow at the top of the wedding cake cliff, or maybe more like sedimentary ice cliff, depending on your level of romanticism, and I realized I was standing, not on solid rock, but on ten feet of ice that had grown up over the winter from snowfall and waterfall spray.

At the far end of the trail there was nothing. Wide open plains of snow with little hills in the distance, truly empty and wild country. The featureless landscape was like a virtual reality where they haven't finished creating the simulation. There are many places like this in Iceland, or maybe it's fairer to say that there are fewer actual places and more emptiness in that land than I have ever experienced before.

I took my Yaris south through the emptiness, stopping briefly at a crater filled with water, like a tiny model of Crater Lake in Oregon. Then farther south to the black sands of the North Atlantic. The snow had melted and there were brown seagrasses in the black sand and green fields which began behind the dunes and ended at the feet of the snowy ridge of mountains I had driven out of.

Looking south over the grey, crashing surf, I suddenly felt very far away from home. If I got in a boat and started paddling due south, I wouldn't hit land until I reached Antarctica over ten thousand miles away. The immensity of the ocean and the tininess of the land I was standing on were suddenly in sharp contrast with each other.

The road led my tiny car back into the low mountains where the snow got thicker and the landscape softened as the rocks disappeared under frozen fluff. Soon the road merged with a four lane highway and merged again with another, busier road with more cars and trucks and I was back to Reykjavik where I had been working all week with Landsbankinn.

In 2008 Iceland's experiment with privatized banking fell apart. They apparently thought the whole mortgage-backed security thing was a pretty good idea and invested heavily. Then the house of housing cards fell apart and Iceland's banks failed.

I had always said that if I met anyone from Iceland I would feel an obligation to apologize as an American for the stupidity of our country, even though I got screwed by the deal when my retirement evaporated in the stock market crash and later when Citibank illegally foreclosed on my house... At least it was the banking system in my own country that screwed me over.

And here I was in Iceland meeting with the National Bank. I, somewhat sheepishly, mentioned my thoughts about the U.S. banking industry and my feelings about Iceland getting dragged into it, and the guys at Landsbankinn said, "No, our guys went to jail. If it is too good to be true, it probably is, and it's their job to know the difference. It's not America's fault our guys were stupid."

Turns out things really are different in Iceland.

Of course the entire population of Iceland is only about 300,000 people, so fixing the economy was a quicker process because it involved fewer people. They actually have a dating app that includes genealogy so you can avoid dating someone who is too close a cousin. And almost half those people live in Reykjavik, which still makes the city only about 120,000 people, or about the size of Peoria, Illinois.

Meanwhile around 700,000 people visit Iceland every year. Which makes it easier to see why the economy bounced back so fast. More than twice the number of people who live in Iceland pay taxes in Iceland when they shop, rent cars, pay for lodging, and enjoy the splendor of the Northern Lights in a bus tour.

The shopping districts and the restaurants and the concert halls probably wouldn't exist without the constant flow of tourists, let alone things like Universal Health Care. Now, if we can just get 600 million people to visit the U.S...

Even though I was in Iceland for business, I took the tour bus from Reykjavik to the Blue Lagoon the first day I arrived. It had only been a nine-hour travel day for me, short compared to my normal fifteen-hour days from Portland to anywhere in Europe, and I figured a soak in the hot seawater would be a good way to work the kinks out of my cramped, travel-weary muscles.

There wasn't much to see on the drive out to the lagoon. Snow-covered lava fields with bits of moss poking through. As we got close I saw some sort of industrial building with a plume of steam that I later learned was a geothermal plant. All of Iceland's power is geothermal, which meant my laptop charging at the hotel was storing the power of a volcano in its little battery.

Then pools of bright water started to appear in the lava fields. Like so many Southern California swimming pools dropped in the middle of nowhere, the bright aquamarine pools stood out in high contrast against the dark basalt.

The bus dropped us in a parking lot surrounded by a wall of lava rocks that must have been pushed aside when they leveled the lot. Following the parade of tourists down a paved path through the man-made canyon of lava rocks, I crossed a bridge over another pool and found myself in the lobby of a resort. While there are thermal pools outside the resort, you have to stick to the enclosed area, which means paying for entry.

The sleet was blowing sideways and icy water clung to my beard, but the water was hot enough to balance out the cold. The soaking lagoon, filled with seawater that is pushed up from the ground by volcanic heat, is maybe a quarter of an acre with outcroppings of rough rock poking above the surface here and there.

It's not entirely natural -- the hot water itself is wastewater from the geothermal plant, which isn't something they advertise. So, it isn't really a "spring" so much as a "pump" as they push seawater into the ground and condense steam as it comes back out, but it's clean, hot, briny water that makes you feel like a Viking as you soak below and freeze above.

The enormous pool is coated with cement, creating a smooth lining. Without the cement slathered inside the pools the surface would be jagged lava which can cut like an evil, serrated blade. Having customers bleed to death is bad for business in any culture.

I found myself in a small pool to one side out of the wind and where hot water welled up from a vent. Sometimes I would get hot enough to hoist myself up onto the ledge and let the Icelandic sleet bring my temperature back down before slipping back into the water.

A bevy of British women on a holiday tour package was keeping me company. They were there to see the Northern Lights and were a bit disappointed to find out that I wasn't going to be on their bus tour for the next few days.

I made a mental note that if I found myself single with a bit of time and extra money on my hands to book in for one of those tours. As unlikely that combination is ever to be, being surrounded by wet, English women in the hot waters of the Blue Lagoon was a fantasy I'm surprised I had never constructed for myself.

After the soaking, after a shower, after an amazingly expensive lunch, I braved the weather and took a walk around the outside of the resort in the "real" lagoons, which were, honestly, very much like the lagoons inside the resort -- the lava is the same rough rock and the aquamarine color comes from the minerals in the water, not a painted lining.

As I rode back to Reykjavik I wondered if the landscape had changed much with the introduction of the geothermal plant and its mineral laden waters or if there had been, at one time, Vikings soaking in small natural pools. Probably not, as the pools are all drainage for the plant, but the visual would make a great beer commercial.

The problem with dining in Reykjavik is that there are only two kinds of restaurants. There is Domino's Pizza and Subway for the locals taking a lunch break, and the next step up are epic restaurants for the tourists. That first night I had an appetizer board with grilled meats including puffin and whale. Like an American buying a Cuban cigar in the Caribbean, this was one of those "well, it's legal here" moments.

The puffin reminded me of turkey, and the whale reminded me of beef, making me think of that bit in *The Matrix* when they were wondering how the computers know what things taste like, and maybe that's why so many things taste alike -- if my trip to Iceland was really a virtual reality simulation, they could have just tweaked the "beef" setting with a little seawater and called it "whale."

The second night was venison and an amazing French Bordeaux in a little restaurant tucked away in the modern, cavernous, glass and concrete, yet somehow aesthetically pleasing Harpa Concert and Conference Center. The light jazz in the background caught my ear as I picked out the melodies.

"Excuse me," as I caught the waiter's attention. "Is that jazz actually Madonna? And was that The Clash just before?" Apparently no one had ever commented on the obscure YouTube mix of '80's hits covered as dinner jazz.

By the third night I was dreading yet another epic meal. I was beginning to understand why celebrity chefs are dodgy when asked, "What's your favorite meal?" At some point foie gras and delicate pastries become humdrum and your body starts to crave mac and cheese.

But I ended up with sushi. It was a Japanese fusion bar in the basement of a two-hundred-year-old warehouse and I ended up with something they called "sushi pizza" which I washed down with Korean soju. It was amazing, though -- two sheets of nori fried in tempura batter with locally caught Arctic char sashimi and a delicate asian sauce.

Meanwhile I was having epic breakfasts. Iceland does the same meats, fish and cheeses I had come to like in Norway and Sweden, although there were a few more sweets on the breakfast bar, undoubtedly for the American pallet.

When I had told my friends I was going to Iceland I consistently got the response, "Oh! Iceland! I've always wanted to go there!" It confused me because I didn't get the same kind of response when I went to Dusseldorf or Trondheim, and in many ways Reykjavik is just another European city.

Yes, there are amazing things to see in Iceland, but there is also a lot of empty landscape of old, brown lava rock, maybe covered in moss making it an expanse of green rock, maybe covered in snow making it an expanse of white rock. But for the most part, Iceland is an expanse of rock with a nice little city dropped on it.

I'm not saying I didn't enjoy Reykjavik, but I live in a city with epic meals and art galleries and interesting shopping. And I'm not saying there is anything wrong with an expanse of rocky landscapes, but I have those in driving distance from my house, and I have driven, ridden and hiked those open, rocky spaces. We have volcanic hot springs just up the road and crashing surf just down the road.

There are even Toyota Yarises and British tourists in Portland.

Foreign Lands

The brown hills outside of Madrid looked almost exactly like the brown hills in the South Bay near San Jose. So much so that I posted a photo on Facebook and asked my friends to tell me what part of California they thought I was in.

On the drive up to the client's office I passed Mercedes dealerships, an IKEA and of course there were McDonald's and Starbucks scattered throughout the city. I couldn't understand a word the driver said, but that's often true in California, too.

Most of my travel is for business, so I don't find myself on the Serengeti or deep in the interior of Australia. I stay in European-style hotels and visit companies that regularly do business with U.S. companies. So I suppose I shouldn't expect my international travels to be National Geographic wonders.

Even so, as I rode through rush hour traffic on a Madrid freeway in the back of the four-door Skoda made in Germany by Volkswagen, I began to wonder if I had started my world travels too late and that I was fated to traveling a familiar world of multinational brands that would blur my memory of the places I had been until I couldn't distinguish Madrid from Dusseldorf or Atlanta.

Tokyo

THE TYPHOON RAINS HAD KEPT THE CROWDS AWAY AND I HAD the Imperial Gardens practically to myself. The ancient walls framed the immaculate gardens giving me the feeling of being four hundred years in the past in the Edo period, other than the modern buildings of Tokyo towering above the garden's massive embattlement walls like some failure in the projection of a nearly perfect holographic illusion.

The occasional English translations didn't always help me know what I was seeing. *Site of Matsunoohroka Corridor* only means something to me if I know what "Matsunoohroka" is referring to and Google couldn't help me.

The phonetic English didn't match up to anything and I could Google and I couldn't look up Kanji in a phrasebook. I thought Germany was tough with those weird words like "süßigkeit," but at least I generally figured out stuff from context in Dusseldorf.

But there is no context if you don't understand any of the characters and you don't have any way to enter them into a smartphone anyway.

Even if I was oblivious to momentous history as I walked through the garden, the sense of foreignness was reinforced by the indecipherable signs in the large, immaculate gardens. The occasional medieval stone wall or large wooden building with rice paper windows dripping rainwater from the recent deluge made me feel I really was truly in Japan.

I took pictures like a Japanese tourist... well, I suppose I took pictures like an American tourist, everything is at least a little different in Japan. The walls, the trees and the ancient pagodas shrouded in fog and drizzle are some of my favorite photos from my trips that year, although I have to admit I took a much better photo of a bonsai tree in Madrid a couple of weeks before.

My traveling had gotten me accustomed to being eight or ten hours in the future, but Japan was different. I had to keep reminding myself that it wasn't an eight hour time difference, but, really, a sixteen hour time difference. I got online at three in the afternoon on Monday after working with clients all morning, only to find my friends and family were still living in Sunday night, posting complaints about having to go to bed so they could go to work Monday... The Monday I just finished.

I had flown in from Portland the day before; the flight was just like the flight from Portland to Amsterdam, spending ten hours living in a tiny tube suspended in nothingness over an ocean that I only assumed was somewhere below us. Although the sun we were chasing blazed for the entire flight, the blinds were closed and the lights were dim -- like putting a blanket over the canary cage, flight attendants prefer their passengers to believe it is the middle of the night and just go to sleep.

Narita is part of the United Federation of Airports, but the familiarity fades quickly as you exit the secure part of the airport and start to look for ground transportation. The woman at the desk tried to understand my pronunciation of "Sheraton Miyako" and I tried to understand her response.

I finally pulled out my phone and handed it to her with my reservation information; she then took my credit card and gave me a ticket and a number for the area to stand.

The sun had won the race across the Pacific and I stood in the muggy, October evening air inside the lines of a painted area, reminding me of the box you are told to stand in while you wait to be booked into jail.

I boarded the bus with some confusion about whether it was even the right bus, found a seat and listened to what sounded like dire warnings about something or other in Japanese and then a lovely female voice with just enough mix of Japanese and English accents to be cute reminded me to fasten my seatbelt and not to smoke.

The lights were bright inside the bus, and I couldn't really see much out the windows. The warm air, bright lights, stop and go, and the smells of perfume and diesel exhaust were almost too much for my jetlagged, sleep-deprived body, but I managed to get to the hotel without having an embarrassing carsick moment.

The Sheraton Miyako caters to American and European travelers, with the basic hotel room layout that was cut from a pattern forty years ago and is a constant in a world of change. Of course the toilets have all the buttons for bidet and heated seat functions, all of which I carefully avoided having heard the stories of bidet water in the face. The TV shows were all in Japanese and I needed to stay awake a little longer to get on local time, so I headed to the bar.

The spacious lobby bar was scattered with deep couches facing a two-story-tall wall of windows overlooking the hotel's private garden. While looking at the tapas selection and listening to a jazz duo playing *Moon River* on piano and bass, the surrealism of my travels caught up with me.

Two weeks before I was sitting in a café on a plaza in Madrid with a couple of Belgian colleagues, a week before that I was having an amazing meal in a tiny town in rural Pennsylvania. I know my travel isn't normal, but it wasn't the culture shock that got me on my first night in Tokyo, it was the lack of it. I had a strong sense of deja vu; or maybe, in one sense, I really had been here before...

Back in the late nineties when we were just getting off modems and onto DSL, I would stream the live recordings of a jazz group that played every Friday night in a Tokyo bar -- of course, I was living in Portland, but the Internet lets you do that sort of thing. Maybe it wasn't this bar, but I had heard the same style of jazz from Japan, and I had stayed in the same style of hotel, and I had just had tapas in a place very far away.

My deja vu was shattered the next day. This may have been a Sheraton but it was definitely Japan. I tried the "traditional breakfast" my first morning -- pickled and dyed vegetables, rice, miso and that Japanese delicacy that has the consistency of chunky phlegm, natto. The waitress was surprised and happily impressed that I ate natto (enough soy sauce can make anything go down), and while the pickles and the tea and miso were tasty, I admit, I ate the rest of my breakfasts that week at the European buffet.

This was one of my few trips where I had family in the far away place I was visiting. My niece, Kyra, had married her Japanese beau, Takeshi, and they had settled in Tokyo.

They came by the hotel with baby Ray and picked me up in Takeshi's Subaru Legacy B4 2.0GT -- a nice car anywhere, but more so in Tokyo. Car ownership in Tokyo is kind of a big deal, you have to prove you have off-street parking before you can buy it, and then there are the taxes and the gas and the parking and the licensing and... Well let's just say that Takeshi is rightfully proud of the car and I didn't really realize at the time what a treat it was to get out on the roads.

And those roads are crowded, even on a Sunday morning. The elevated freeway felt like a log flume, as it snaked through the mixture of tall buildings and traffic changed quickly making things even more chaotic as my brain kept trying to flip from right to left-handed driving rules.

Then the torrential downpour started, the kind of thick and heavy rain that is normally created by Hollywood special effects crews. The thunderous noise on the pavement was loud enough to drown out the sounds of Tokyo.

We were on our way to the fish market at Tsukiji, but a day in the shopping mall suddenly seemed like a much better idea than the outdoors. Tokyo Station is exactly what you do not picture when you think "shopping mall" in the U.S. Long hallways connecting with other hallways that feel more like office corridors than a shopping center. The rain had driven everyone inside, and in Tokyo that's a lot of "everyone."

The windowless corridors lined with windowless shops went on forever, in every direction, with packed escalators and packed stores and packed walkways. It was hard to say when we were above ground or when we were below ground, and it probably didn't matter.

After lunch and a visit to the banana vending machine, just to prove they exist (the machines, not bananas), we escaped the crowds and I said goodbye to Kyra, Takeshi and Baby Ray, and then I braved the train system back to my hotel.

That sense of being illiterate hit me again as I stood in front of the machine trying to figure out which train to take. Yes, the signs were printed in both Japanese and English, for the most part. It's that "for the most part" that was the real problem -- some trains weren't listed in English and an entire train line was indecipherable.

Precise but broken English interrupted my study of the rail map. "May I help? You... sir?" and I found a middle-aged businesswoman suddenly by my side. Her English wasn't that good, but it was English and she tried to help me figure out which platform I had to go to.

There seems to be a generation of Japanese who were taught to help foreigners, especially at the train -- maybe it's part of practicing English, maybe it's being a good host, but there seemed something formal and practiced about the interaction. No matter what her reasons, she did help me get on the right train.

I was surprised to find walls with doors lining the edge of the platform. I assume this is to keep the crush of people from inadvertently pushing waiting passengers onto the tracks and under the wheels of the train.

On a Sunday when there was hardly anyone out this wasn't a problem, but later in the week I met with my colleague from Malaysia, who spoke enough Japanese to get around town and we took the train in the rush-hour crush. I didn't see the men with the white gloves who pack you into a train car, but it was tight. Being over six feet tall helped a lot by putting me a head above most of the other passengers, but there are plenty of tall Japanese these days.

CK may have known some Japanese, but he insisted on carrying on our conversation on the train. We think of the Japanese as overly polite with strict social rituals, rituals most Americans can't fathom. But the idea that you should shut up on the train makes sense to me when you're in a car at 200 percent capacity.

That silence is, however, almost creepy as the masses of workers all head to work. Standing in Shinagawa Station, I stood to the side and watched as they marched through the wide terminal, no one talking, everyone dressed in dark suits and ties with white shirts and heading in the same direction toward the office complex behind the station. Knowing there was a slaughterhouse just beyond those office towers made my brain twist in uncomfortable ways.

I joined the procession because my meetings were in those same office towers. The day was much like other days, standing in front of a room, talking about products and strategy and industry trends and all the other things that get wrapped up into the ball of "knowledge transfer" that I do.

Except it wasn't really transferring.

The Japanese like to pretend they speak English, and they certainly speak more of it than I speak Japanese. They were constantly surprised by my command of Japanese when it came to food, "You know oyakodon?!?" Growing up on the Pacific Rim meant having to learn how to order in Japanese restaurants, so yes, I know oyakodon.

But when you get away from chicken and eggs over rice there are concepts that are hard to get, even if you're a native speaker. They were too polite to interrupt and ask for clarification, so my Japanese colleague told me the trick -- give them permission to talk to each other.

Things went better after that, with chatter that I couldn't understand, but a process I could follow as I saw them going from utter confusion to finding the light switch and the bulb lighting up over their heads.

Then came the drinking.

I admit, I was worried about the drinking in Tokyo. I had heard tales of the after-work drinking in Japanese business culture, and about the special train cars for women to keep the drunken gropings by businessmen at bay. I had to make it through a solid week of lecturing to Japanese tech guys and I didn't want to do it hung over.

I shouldn't have been worried. I was, after all, in constant training for events like these. I live in a part of the world known for massive quantities of strong beer. I had kept up with the Brits in polite drinking competitions. I had downed the 1-litre glasses of Uerige alt in Germany. I had braved aquavit in Norway. I was ready.

And they... they were not.

Three mugs of Suntory lager, tops, and they were sloppy drunks. We sat on the tatami mats in a private room, a table surrounded by shoji screens, the walls lined with black suit jackets on hangers. The beer flowed; I knew the ritual of filling the other guys' glasses but never filling my own glass and they did a good job of filling mine.

Their English got worse, but I had my surprise cultural references to Kyary Pamyu Pamyu ("Pon pon way pon pon!") and Ultraman (a little pantomime of the superhero's hand position as he shoots rays of death) and language mattered less and less as everyone laughed and slapped the table.

The party broke up, I took a cab back to the Sheraton and had a scotch and listened to the evening's jazz ensemble, hardly touched by a buzz of alcohol.

Every day that week followed a similar flow. One day I was in a tiny room with too many people and too little air and in one of those breaks where they explained to each other what I meant, I looked behind the curtain at the endless concrete landscape of Tokyo. From the 45th floor the city looked like the Goblin King's Labyrinth, with the twisting streets and mish-mash of buildings, and just a touch of craziness where a roller coaster inexplicably climbed out of the landscape.

Then came another special meal with beer and wine. I have to admit the shabu-shabu experience makes me understand why people go to Benihana, the same way I understand why people drink cheap wine, because it reminds them of the good stuff. Shabu-shabu in Japan is the good stuff.

Leaving the restaurant that night I saw a rare sight in Tokyo -- a big black man. The product he was pitching was simple, the girls were probably just as friendly as he said, but he dropped his sales act and we were Americans for a moment, talking without editing for non-English speakers, a sincere, "Hang in there, man" and even a quick fist bump, just because it seemed natural, and there was precious little that seemed natural to me in Tokyo.

Saturday rolled around and I packed up and went to meet Kyra and family at Shibuya Station. I again had the problem of deciphering the signs but eventually got on the right platform and the right train. The pleasant female voice announced each stop in English and the LED signs rolled by in Kanji and English, but I still had that feeling that I could get absolutely lost at any second and I watched anxiously for both "Shibuya" and the string of characters I had memorized that I believed to mean "Shibuya Station" but could have equally meant "movie theater" or "asylum."

Shibuya is another huge underground complex that passes for a rail station in Tokyo. I found a locker to store my suitcase and gear and tried to find my way out of the labyrinth of the station, somehow emerging on the upper deck of a mezzanine, having overshot the ground floor as I fought my way to the surface.

Everywhere I looked there were jumbotrons and giant signs and shops and umbrellas... It was exactly like being in Times Square only completely different.

The diagonal zebra crossing swarming with umbrellas led to a Starbucks topped with a six-story-tall glass of beer slowly being filled. The intersection was once again tickling my deja vu; it seems every TV show and movie ever filmed in Japan by Westerners has a scene in this crosswalk.

As I tried to find my way into Starbucks I wandered through the multi-story music and movie store. Paul McCartney's new album was coming out that day and there was a queue out to the street with people waiting to buy it. There were rooms and rooms of DVDs and rooms for CDs and for audio cables and for video adapters...

I had begun to learn that Japan isn't ten years ahead of us, as I had always thought, but that they are living ten years in the past.

The iPhone has begun to catch on, but half of Japan still uses the "gala-kei" or "Galapagos" phone; phones that have evolved in their own, isolated island of Japan like the animals of the Galapagos Islands with features filling niches in their environment. A gala-kei phone can pay for a train ticket by touching the gate sensor but there's no Starbuck's app.

The world of smartphones in Japan is still a ways off and the Japanese people still flock to the stores to buy physical media. This wasn't just foreign because it was Japan, it was foreign to the modern age I live in.

Of course, it's not all 1990's tech and I was able to communicate with Kyra using our 21st century equivalent of telepathy -- Facebook Messenger. I frequently find myself in Starbucks when I'm in faraway lands, not for the coffee but because they have free WiFi, and I was able to get online, connect and vaguely describe my location. I really don't know how people traveled before WiFi...

The endless loop of the techno-Halloween music about crazy, crazy cats dancing and scary, scary pumpkins that was sung in heavily Japanese-accented English tortured me from a TV in the corner of the novelty/housewares store, Loft, a store that will forever be "Loft-o" to me because of the way Japanese throw an "o" after a word ending with a consonant.

Halloween had come to Tokyo; I don't know why the Japanese hadn't embrace Halloween earlier, Japan being the home of Cosplay and all. But now that Halloween is there, it's getting big. Not with kids, it's more like Santa Con, where people take the opportunity to completely break from sanity.

After I reached my Tokyo shopping limit, we took the train to Kyra and Takeshi's neighborhood in Nerima. The jumble of buildings on twisting narrow streets formed a chaotic backdrop outside the window as we sped along the elevated tracks. Then came our stop and we descended into that chaos.

Mind you, the streets are much easier to navigate than crazy places like Bangalore; traffic flows at a regular pace, and stops for traffic lights. The fact they drive on the left side of the street is only slightly disorienting. Of course that's only true on the big streets -- there is no side to drive on when you get into the narrow alleys that are side streets off the main drag.

The neighborhood was a cluster of four and five-story buildings that crowded the narrow streets with a tangled web of electrical and communications cables crisscrossing overhead, making the streets feel even smaller, as if the cables might be tightened and pull the buildings even closer together like the strings of a corset.

Kyra and Takeshi had a huge apartment by Tokyo standards; I can't really remember how big because apartments are measured by the number of tatami mats they can fit, but even with the spare bedroom it couldn't have been much more than 500 square feet. But, hey, spare bedroom in Tokyo.

Takeshi and I were sitting on the couch watching the latest *Top Gear* episodes (which wouldn't air in the U.S. for a few more months) and in a quiet spot where Jeremy Clarkson wasn't yelling or crashing into something, I heard singing outside the window. Kyra said, "It's the Yam Man!"

Takeshi and I gathered up and rushed to the street like kids catching the ice cream truck before it slipped away, although I doubt you would get kids to chase down a man selling roasted yams in the U.S.

In the dark alleyway, a small pickup truck sat with speakers playing a recording of a woman singing her siren yam call. The song reminded me of *Blade Runner* where floating advertisements with a singing Chinese woman drifted over the city, but the setting here was completely different.

This was residential Tokyo. Quiet. Dark. No one on the streets except for Takashi, me and the yam seller. The yams were wrapped in foil and were slowly roasting in a compartment that formed a wood-burning oven in the back of the truck. The yam man opened the firebox so I could see and the warm glow of the flames nearly blinded me in the otherwise dimly-lit street.

We took our yams back to the apartment and I watched Ray get his first taste of warm yam. He was just starting to eat solid food and once he got a taste, he tried to get his mom to feed him a yam the size of his head. Maybe kids do chase down the Yam Man in Tokyo...

I slept on the futon on the floor of their spare room that night, with the glow of my phone charging from from my laptop that was slightly out of reach, causing me to wake up more than I normally would as I tried to check the time, only to find I had to crawl halfway across the small room to see the numbers on my phone.

Soon it was time again to pack up and head to the airport. Heading back by train seemed much less daunting after a week of Tokyo trains, although when changing trains I had another middle-aged business person ask in formal tones if I needed help as I stared dumbly at the board, trying to figure out which platform I was supposed to be on.

The Narita Express rushed through the city, and then out into the countryside, which looked a lot like Oregon with rolling green fields, occasional subdivisions, power lines and roads. It was much more peaceful and comfortable than the drive into town had been my first night, and, almost too soon, I was at the end of the line where I reentered the familiar, comforting world of the UFA.

I was worried about the bottle of soju Takeshi had recommended because I didn't know if there was a customs restriction. As I checked in at the Delta counter the women giggled as if I had confided a secret to them ("Ahhhhhh! Soju!") as they placed "fragile" stickers all over my bag, more concerned that my liquor made it safely home than whether I was breaking any international law.

The only thing I had promised Markie was that I would bring her green tea Kit Kats, something Kyra had brought to us on an earlier trip, and I was heading home empty-handed after vainly searching Tokyo supermarkets and making Kyra and Takeshi explain it to countless clerks. But every airport is like exiting through the gift shop at the end of the museum tour -- there was a big display of Matcha Kit Kats in the shop right by my gate.

So, with liquor and candy, a million photos and probably an extra pound or two from all the business sponsored meals, I headed home from one of the most exotic places on my travels, but certainly not the most, because my job is in Technology. And the capital of Tech is in India.

Bangalore

IT WAS SOMEWHERE AROUND TWO IN THE MORNING AS THE CAR danced in traffic on the rough road into Bangalore. The familiar belt and sword of Orion glowed on the horizon and I found myself thinking of that scene in *Roots* when Fanta asked Kunta Kinte if it was the same moon in this new place.

"Everything about this new place is different, so why wouldn't the moon be different also?"

The shops in London feel like the shops in New York, which feel like the shops in Tokyo. But there is no question that you are somewhere different when you are in India. The smell of spice and smoke and a billion people is in the air when you step off the plane. The men in uniforms carry rifles and look at you from under their hats as if you are an alien being and they aren't sure if you are a threat or not.

I found myself standing in a wide, empty section of floor just outside the security area. On the other side of the expanse was a sea of men in slacks and button-up shirts and women in colorful dresses and scarves all holding placards with names -- no one who arrives by air in Bangalore rents a car and drivers with cars are cheap, which meant I had to find my driver among hundreds of others.

Other Westerners and I banded together, all in the same predicament -- finding my particular driver was like trying to find your winter coat in the bedroom of a particularly well-attended party. I scanned for a placard with my name on it, calling to the other travelers or they would call to me, "Is that your name?" Our numbers shrank and grew again as people found their drivers and new visitors emerged from security until I eventually found a tall youngish man holding an almost legible sign that said something like "M~ B;s~~"

My driver led me out into the warm smoky air of India, across the eternal traffic jam in front of the terminal and had me wait on the sidewalk as he went to get the car. Cars came and went and people came and went with them. I could see smoke rising just beyond the parking area -- I never found out what was burning, but soon learned there's always smoke rising somewhere nearby, maybe a national incense burn to add to the pungent air.

Eventually it was my turn to sit in the back of a car as it barely moved through the lanes of traffic leading from the airport. The giant billboards loomed darkly by the roadside, unlit at this hour because the cost of electricity outweighs an advertising opportunity.

Traffic was heavy but, unlike in the daytime in Bangalore, it was moving, even though we probably never got above 30 mph. The road was under construction, and the car had to slow for sudden zigzags that routed us from new pavement to old pavement or to no pavement at all.

The hired cars jockeyed for position like rally drivers, coming within inches of each other as they fought for holes in traffic that only existed for fractions of seconds. Heavily loaded trucks trundled slowly down the road while cars swooped around them to the constant sound of the {*beep*}{*beep*} of horns.

Constant honking is less of the American blaring, "Get the hell out of my way!" and more of an, "Excuse me," in India. It is not only polite, but many of the trucks solicit beeps with signs like, "*Please 'honk' when passing*," as if overloaded trucks will be able to manoeuvre better if they know a sedan is about to barrel by.

Occasionally I would see a car or a truck on the side of the road, hood open or the axle precariously balanced on a stack of rocks while a group of men stood around staring at it, undoubtedly having the same kinds of conversations men have standing around broken-down vehicles everywhere.

And everywhere there were dogs.

Medium sized dogs with brown, short hair, all cut from the same breed were slinking through the streets looking for food. These are "village dogs," never domesticated or bred like our Chihuahuas and Great Danes; the wild ancestors of these dogs learned how to live with humans without becoming pets. You see them sometimes in the daytime, sleeping in the sun, but for the most part they come out at night and then disappear when the city wakes.

I tried to keep an idea of where I was and where we were going during the hour-long ride through the dark urban landscape of Bangalore, but as we passed through the city itself, the turns became more frequent and it seemed we were shooting down alleys and side streets more often than being on the main road. I still wonder if there even is a main road through Bangalore.

Eventually we reached the gates of my hotel. A guard ran a mirror under the car and checked the trunk before we were allowed to drive the final 30 feet to the front door where I was then asked to put my bags through an X-ray machine before entering the lobby.

I'm not sure what they are guarding against. The Mecure doesn't seem like a likely target for terrorist attacks, but like the farmer banging his sticks to keep elephants out of the trees in the U.S. it seemed to be working. ("How do you know it works?" "You don't see any elephants in the trees do you?")

The hallways were like other hotel hallways although there was a lone goldfish in a bowl to greet me as I stepped off the elevator. Everywhere I went in Bangalore there were scents and smells. I don't know if the hotel used one of those scent machines like the ones they use in Vegas casinos or not, but there was a distinct, sharp, almost perfume smell throughout the hotel.

After I figured out the electrical outlets (there were European and UK outlets but no U.S.) and plugged my laptop in and my phone into my laptop, I showered and went to bed in a room that was almost too cool, set, no doubt, for Western visitors like myself.

I woke up around eight in the morning the next day; the 27-hour trip seemed to have canceled out the 12 ½-hour time change. In all my time travels, the India time difference is one of the trickier ones. Rather than splitting the country into two time zones, they split the difference, so they're five and a half hours off from Universal Time (what we used to call GMT). Scheduling conference calls is particularly tricky, but that's why we have computers that take care of that kind of math for us.

Breakfast at the Bangalore Mecure was a buffet with a mix of European and Indian choices and while I tried some of the dumplings and sauces from the Indian side of the buffet, I made my real breakfast from grilled tomatoes, fried eggs and toast with fruit. There were bananas and oranges, and there were other fruits I had never seen before or since -- some things just don't ship thousands of miles.

I sat in the walled garden under awnings that kept the warm, February sun at bay as I watched a cook manning the crepe and waffle bar near the artificial waterfall. The tiny bells from the Buddhist temple next door tinkled over the wall while I sipped coffee and caught up on news and friends on my laptop. The place made me think of the garden that Chauncey Gardiner tended in *Being There,* except I knew that there was a very different world over that wall.

My hotel was only a few blocks from the office and I needed a walk, so I thought I might see some of that world over the wall. International travel would be a completely different experience without Google Maps -- I like to think I have a decent sense of direction, but the streets aren't exactly on a grid in that part of the world. I can imagine using a compass and a protractor on a paper map in the urban wilderness of Bangalore.

A couple of motor scooters zipped by as I stepped through the hotel gates and into the small street. Down the way there was a man pushing a giant cart piled with cloth. The not-quite feral village dogs lazed in the sun after another night of scavenging.

The lot next to the hotel was a pile of rubble from either an old building or a construction project that never got done. It seemed there was a family living in one of the rocky abandoned construction sites, the kids crawling around the chunks of broken concrete like a playground. And the smoke was everywhere from people cooking or burning trash or old fires that never seem to go out.

I almost gave up and asked for a car after standing there for a few seconds trying to process everything that I was seeing, hearing and smelling. But I tightened up the strap of my messenger bag, checked the map on my phone and headed down the street.

The small side street emptied into a bigger street, packed with cars and motorcycles and the "auto rickshaws," essentially a three-wheeled motorcycle with a cab on it that serves as the main taxi service in India. The British influence shows in the street signs with Keep Left, but the traffic doesn't seem to follow a clear left or right side of the street, instead pushing into whatever empty space it can find.

Crossing the street feels like taking your life into your hands. The cross traffic flows for as long as it can until the stopped traffic just can't take it any longer and pushes its way into the intersection, taking the right of way. Traffic flows until the pattern is reversed again when the other street retakes the intersection.

Whatever the unspoken rule is that says how long is long enough seems to work, but I always expected to see a collision that never happened. The fact that traffic never gets much faster than fifteen miles an hour might help avoid brutal accidents, but the sheer volume of traffic makes it seem impossible that there aren't toppled vehicles every ten feet.

Being a tall white guy, I stood out in the crowd. Something about sunglasses made me even more visible -- when I wore them people stopped and stared at the bearded, sunglass-wearing American, which must have made me look either like a movie star or a hit man. Without them, people still looked, but with just a glance and then they moved on.

I tried walking on the sidewalks, and soon discovered they weren't really sidewalks at all. The large concrete pavers were sometimes missing or badly cracked and I could see below into a ditch or storm drain. The thought of misstepping and falling into the cavern below made the thought of dancing in and out of traffic less unappealing.

Some of the buildings had signs on them with familiar tech companies like Wipro or Accenture. But for the most part I couldn't tell what was what. A large unmarked building had uniformed guards out front and could have been a shop, or a consulate, or a private home. It seemed that having a man in a military-style uniform in front of your building was a status symbol or maybe a design detail like a lawn jockey.

The nondescript building that was my office was tucked away off the main drag behind another rubble-filled lot. There were no signs on the building, but there were uniformed guards. The guards smiled and buzzed me in, apparently my Western features were enough to prove that I had business in the building.

The space was almost like a giant cafeteria with laptops everywhere. I knew people in this office both from working with them in the U.S. and virtually, having worked on projects with them for years yet never meeting ("Vinit! My brother!") and soon I found a space where I could sit and get online and email the people who were now only 20 feet away.

As the jet lag crept in, I found my screen blurring and my head getting heavy so I got directions to the kitchen for coffee. While India is not as caste-driven as in the past, there are still cultures within cultures. The group of people in the kitchen were there to serve me my coffee -- when I tried to get it myself I was given a scolding stare, and I quickly relinquished my cup. I don't know if it is because the work is beneath me or if it is because I'm not qualified to pour a cup of coffee, but either way, it simply is not done.

The mug was like any corporate mug -- white enamel and our company logo, but the coffee was definitely not corporate coffee.

Southern Indian coffee is brewed slowly in large urns and comes out as a thick, viscous liquor that Eva Gabor's *Green Acres* character would have been proud of. The mug is filled maybe halfway with coffee and from a second urn they top it off with steaming sweet milk. This isn't like when I get a latte at Starbucks and I'm trying to drown the bitter flavor -- this is the promise of coffee fulfilled where the aroma and the flavor are almost one.

I have tried, in vain, to find this coffee in the US, but it is never the same. They probably don't use goat's milk in the U.S., but I'm sure the coffee beans are different and the water is different. But I really think it's more like how amazing S'mores are when you're camping but not the same when you make them in a toaster oven at home. It's a bit of being in the time and place that makes it so fantastic.

With nirvana in a corporate mug I returned to my desk. The weather in Bangalore in February is like Southern California, fairly dry but warm. Long fabric tubes stretched overhead from one wall to the other and delivered a gentle breeze from the air conditioning system.

My colleagues didn't react as the lights went out and the brightly colored air ducts collapsed. Power supply in India is inconsistent, and a tech company invests in plenty of power backup systems. Our laptops had battery power, the WiFi still worked, the servers were still running, and the large windows let in plenty of daylight. Discussions about clients and products continued with the gentle clatter of typing on keyboards.

[BAM]

I jumped as the violent explosion of the air conditioning ducts reinflating signaled the power was back. Air racing the length of the fabric tubes formed a visible wave as it forced itself through until it hit the end of the duct with a force that shook the entire system. Then the soft hiss of cool air began to drift its way into the room and everything was quiet again.

Lunch was served by the same invisible caste of people who had made my coffee. When I asked my colleagues what the different dishes were they couldn't really answer. Unlike the dishes in Japan which I knew from home, Indian food isn't about the name of the food, but the general flavor. Different sauces and different vegetables, but usually something spicy and something even spicier. Of course, even the sweets seemed spicy to me.

I have been in tech a long time, and I have worked with Indians for an equally long time. I hate it when Americans assume India is about offshore work and substandard call centers. The real tech work that powers our modern economy is done here, and there are some brilliant people doing that work.

And they work hard. Granted, they come in around ten in the morning, but they stay late, often midnight -- the time zone means the rest of the world starts working about noon, India time, and calls are often scheduled for mid-morning in the Pacific time zone, meaning late evening India time.

The company brings in an "afternoon snack" which is more like a second lunch, and often another meal later in the evening and they keep working. Fortunately I was there to work with people on local India time, so I just had to deal with my internal clock, not the rest of the world's clocks.

The official language of India is English, although it's different English than the English governors spoke. Even the TV advertisements have the thick Indian accent that American comedians like to make fun of.

Indians would be hard enough to understand if I was working with normal topics and people who spoke the language the same way I do. But we're talking smart people talking about complex topics with not only a pronunciation difference, but a different set of cultural cues.

Some time after a spicy lunch, I was in a meeting explaining a particularly complicated bit of tech and I had to stop one of my colleagues as he was doing the Indian head bobble, gently rolling his head back and forth.

"Okay, sorry, I'm just going to have to be the dumb American for a moment here," I told him. "Sometimes when I see someone shaking his head like that it means, 'I understand,' and sometimes it means, 'I'm confused...' Which is it?"

Fortunately everyone laughed and he explained he was confused. But Indians are used to people being confused.

Saying, "I've been to India," is like saying, "I've been to the U.S." It's not just one place. India used to be a collection of kingdoms until the British put them all under a central government -- the regional differences are still enormous, far more different than Miami is from Portland.

Bangalore is one of those melting pot cities like Los Angeles where no one is really from there. I didn't get away with not understanding the culture just because I'm from the U.S., they're used to dealing with confused people from other parts of India who also don't know the local lingo or ways and they are almost relieved when you tell them what you don't understand.

At the end of the workday, I braved the traffic in the streets again and wound my way past the guarded buildings and the families living in piles of rubble and back to my hotel. The security guard greeted me by name as he placed my laptop bag in the X-ray machine and I entered the cool, scented air of the Mecure.

In the evenings they closed the hotel pool, liberally sprayed the mosquito repellent, lit the candles and served dinner on the patio by the pool. I balanced my exploring Indian cuisine at the office with more European fare at the hotel; the anglophile in me was looking forward to a little colonial hospitality, which the French-owned hotel was good at providing, except for the striking lack of tonic water. I somehow feel cheated to have never had a G&T under the Indian sun.

The steak and potatoes had a subtle Indian spice to it, whether intentionally or just absorbed from the air but that was nothing compared to the wine. I didn't know that there was local wine produced right there on the Mysore plateau and I had to try it.

Take a heavy grape jelly. Add smoke -- acidic smoke. Then toss in a dash of pepper and vinegar and mix it with antifreeze. I understand now why I had never heard of Indian wine; they probably don't have much of an export business.

I even tried it again a couple of days later thinking my taste buds might have been messed up a bit by the travel and food. Nope. Just the most bizarre wine I've ever had, and I'm including Mr. Johnson's homemade Concord grape wine he made in the back of the feed store in Vacaville in my list of bizarre and horrible wines.

I can't say that I ever got accustomed to Bangalore -- every day was filled with unfamiliar sounds, foods and culture. Unlike most business trips, there wasn't a comfortable, multinational chain store like Starbucks or the lobby of the Hilton. I never felt completely out of sorts, but I never felt entirely comfortable either.

So when it came time to go, I was ready to go. Of course, all flights from Europe seem to come and go in the middle of the night in Bangalore, which meant even leaving was an odd, slip out in the middle of the night affair. I suppose it's one way to start getting on whatever local time you're heading to, and I suppose with India's daytime traffic you would have to leave in the middle of the night to get a midday flight anyhow.

I asked for a wake-up call, and slept for a few hours before getting up at 1 a.m. to be driven back to the airport. The drive back was much like the drive out, only the streets felt empty to me after my adventures in playing in traffic on foot by day.

Usually when I enter an airport I almost feel a sense of relief. I have returned to the rules of the United Federation of Airports. But, to paraphrase Kunta Kinte, "Why wouldn't the airport be different?"

The German woman in line behind me spoke perfect English but didn't understand that she had to go to another line. Men and women have separate screening lines, implying that there may be more than a metal detector or millimeter wave scanner. The loud noises she made in German to her friends could have been humor or rage or a little of both as she expressed her disbelief that she had to resign her place in the men's line and start over in the women's.

Bangalore is one international airport where I don't remember being overwhelmed by the duty-free perfume counters; they may well have been there but the smell of peppers frying in chili oil and an indescribable collection of other spices made the airport smell like a giant kitchen.

Soon I was on board, bag stowed, books and computer ready for the long trip as the flight crew explained the safety procedures in English, French and Dutch. The cabin was closed and the smells and sounds of India were shut out as if I had been beamed aboard a spacecraft and left the planet far behind.

Interlude

The flight was delayed a second time. The plane that was supposed to take us from Atlanta to Charlotte was stuck "Somewhere Else" and Delta was trying to find us another aircraft. I had already spent the first delay in Terminal E at an upscale "southern fusion" restaurant where I had sashimi, pecan pie and a bourbon cocktail with a soy sauce syrup.

They had brought in a second crew; the first crew's day had already worked too many hours and they wouldn't be able to fly, and eventually they got us all boarded. We sat on the tarmac for a while, and then pushed back. And sat some more. I heard the engine revving and holding and I knew that the captain was waiting for a light that had to turn on or turn off to let us fly. A light I knew wasn't going to change.

The captain came on and told us we were heading back to the terminal but that they would get another plane at 11:30 p.m. when it came in. I got off the plane, walked down to the customer service desk and got booked on the 7:30 a.m. flight -- there was no guarantee in my mind that the 11:30 plane would be any more reliable than the 5:30 plane I was supposed to have been on.

I stayed in a Hyatt Place, one of those nondescript hotels that comfort some travelers with their familiarity, but have always made me feel like I was in some lab experiment. My room was 404, which as a web geek I found amusing because that's the error number you get when a page is not found.

The next morning went much better. I got on a half-filled flight, got to the client early enough they didn't even know I had been delayed, and then checked into my hotel. Another Hyatt Place with the same floor plan and fixtures as the one the night before.

I discovered I still had my room key from the previous Hyatt Place, and they said they would just rekey it -- same key system, same cards. And they checked me into Room 404.

Maybe it is a lab experiment...

Epilogue

I NEVER SET OUT TO BE A TRAVELLER. EVEN AFTER WRITING this and revisiting all these places in my mind, I still don't even think of myself as a traveler. And even with all these words describing all these places, I've left out things like the four star restaurant on a ridge in the Rockies that you could only get to by gondola. Or taking the train to Seattle, the ferry to Victoria and a bus to have tea in Butchart Gardens in October. Or walking 28 miles one day and ending up at a pub with showers.

Most places I've been have been because I had to go, but honestly you never have to go anywhere. My mother once asked me why I travel so much if my entire industry is about Internet communications -- I still don't have a good answer for that.

But I think the real answer is because I want to see things, so I find a way to find the opportunity. I want to know that the world isn't a virtual reality simulation or that places like D.C. aren't just fictional lands you only see on TV. If the opportunity to explore a little further is there, I'll take it.

It's not about what you learn on a wiki, on the Travel Channel, or even from reading a book like this, it's about being able to turn your head just a little to one side or the other, looking outside the frame of view -- the tapestry of places and people and things and animals and weather and history and future and every exponential combination isn't something you can capture in words or pictures, because it's only there when you are immersed in it and willing to let yourself be there.

Every waking moment, and many sleeping moments, are "authentic experiences," to steal a phrase from travelogues. Everything you do, even if it's a Big Mac at the drive thru, is a moment in time, and one that is absolutely unique to you, even if it doesn't feel that way.

Stay curious. Be aware. Keep exploring.

Made in the USA
San Bernardino, CA
14 May 2016